Smiley Angels

Love, Peace & Light
Suzanne

By
Suzanne Jennifer Morton

First Published and Printed in May 2007
by Suzanne Jennifer Morton

Reprinted 2008

ISBN: 978 0 9556020 0 9

Printed by: R. Booth Ltd, The Praze, Penryn, Cornwall

Acknowledgements

I would like to thank all my friends and family who have constantly given me help and encouragement to fulfil my ambition of telling the story of the last few years of my life in detail and finally getting it into print.

Special thanks go to my daughters Tracy and Michelle, whose love and affection have provided me with the confidence to completely change my life over the last few years, the story of which forms the basis of this book.

Introduction

I have never considered myself to be a writer, or had any illusions about being a best selling author, and although the first fifty years of my life felt like one long roller-coaster ride, the next few years were to change my life completely and I feel that it is definitely a story worth telling. They say that everyone has a book in them, and as you read mine you will hopefully understand more about what drove me on to write this true story. I hope that you will find it interesting, perhaps touching, but above all inspirational.

Chapter One

Sitting here watching the white waves crashing onto this lovely pale golden beach, seagulls squawking on the roof tops of the charming white cottages and beautiful impressive hotels, it's hard to believe that I now live in this wonderful Cornish town. Yes, Looe has a magic all of its own, in fact, ever since I moved here seven years ago now, I have felt the angels lifting my every step. My life is effortless and opens up more and more each day. I awake each morning filled with joy and happiness, my eyes wide open to the miracles of nature. I'm in love with life itself, and feel that I am in heaven on earth, a place I never thought existed, but how wrong I was. You may wonder how I got to this amazing stage of my life and how I was inspired to move over three hundred miles away from my family and friends, all on my own and without a second thought.

Well, it certainly is a dramatic change from how my life used to be when I lived in Nottinghamshire. Born in 1947 in Ashbourne, Derbyshire, I lived the first year of my life in Matlock and then moved to various towns in Nottinghamshire during the next fifty-two years. I married at nineteen, and in the same year my beautiful daughter Tracy was born. Seven years passed before I gave birth to Michelle in 1974, another beautiful girl. Both have blonde hair in contrast to mine being dark. Unfortunately my marriage did not last and when the girls were twelve and five I started life as a single parent at the age of thirty-two. It was tough, but I learnt a lot about life and it was all part of my journey of self-discovery.

I had a few relationships as the girls got older, but all in all I was happier on my own. When I was in my forties, I used to watch the Oprah Winfrey show and read quite a few of the books she recommended, the first being 'The Road Less Travelled' by M. Scott-Peck, which I read several times. I was doing charity work at the time and was always at my happiest when I was helping people in some way. It made me realise that I had at least got one foot on the right path for me. I also read books by Susan Jeffers and the one that had the most impact on me was "Feel The Fear And Do It Anyway."

Deep down in my heart I never had a sense of belonging in Nottinghamshire at all. I suppose I felt stuck in some sort of rut in a way, but didn't quite know what to do about it. When Tracy was twenty-three she had a baby, my grandson Robert, the apple of my eye, and three years later she got married. It didn't seem long before Michelle had grown up too, and at twenty-two years of age she moved in with Christopher and they were married in February 1998. Christopher is in the Royal Navy and was based in Plymouth, so I suppose it was inevitable that they would move from Nottinghamshire to Devon one day.

It was August 1st 1998 when they finally moved. Very early in the morning, Christopher's father Brian pulled up in a large hired van outside Michelle and Christopher's lovely detached home and they began to load it. Michelle was sobbing because she didn't want to go, and I felt quite numb at the thought of my baby going to live three hundred miles away from me. Michelle, Christopher and Brian waved goodbye as Christopher's mother Carol and I tried to put on a brave face until they were out of sight. When we had vacuumed the carpets for them, we both said a tearful goodbye to each other and went our separate ways. I think I cried for the rest of the day to be honest. Little did I know that it was just the beginning of my new and wonderful life, but the most horrendous bit was to come first. Horrendous hardly seems an adequate word to describe it actually.

A few days went by and Michelle rang from Plymouth to ask if I would go to stay for a few days to help her. So the next day, off I went on the National Express coach to see her. Thousands of fields and cows later, there I was in picturesque Plymouth.

Their home is so lovely and, being at the top of a very steep hill, they are lucky to have the most breathtaking views, stretching for miles on a clear day. Looking out through their dining-room window, white cottages visible through the many trees, their windows twinkling in the distance when the sun shines, you get the feeling that you could well be in Spain, especially at night, when it looks like a magical sight to behold, with the many lights twinkling in the darkness. To the right of their window they can see the sea in the distance. The place gives you a sense of well-being and is very pretty. The two largest bedrooms have king-sized beds and are very tastefully decorated, mine was at the back of the house and had the same view as from the dining-room. The blue and white striped quilt covers and matching curtains complimented the room and made it look very welcoming. It was so welcoming in fact that when I returned again just a few weeks later for a seven week stay, I honestly felt I had died several times in that very room.

During my first visit in August, do bear in mind that with it being a short stay I had not packed much to wear at all, just t-shirts and trousers. Only two days into my stay and still with much to do, Christopher phoned Michelle to say he would be bringing someone home for dinner that evening. Thinking it would be just another one of his mates, I didn't even bother to shower and change before dinner as I was so busy helping Michelle with making the house look nice.

When I was introduced to our dinner guest, it wasn't one of Christopher's mates at all, but a forty-eight year old Naval Officer who was tall, dark and handsome to say the least, and with impeccable manners too. His warm smile revealed perfect white teeth and his whole being just oozing with charisma. It took all my concentration to act as nonchalantly as I did that evening, after deciding about five years previously I felt much better without a man in my life. Each time I looked up at him over the dining room table with the pretty red and blue candles flickering, making him look even more handsome, I thought of my gran and could hear her saying "Stay away from tall, dark, handsome men dear and especially if they appear to be charming too", which of course he was in a shy, quiet, sort of way. After the meal Christopher suggested that we all go down to the pub for 'the last one' as he put it. I prefer to drink water any day rather than anything else, so I pointed out that I could not see the logic in going to the pub when they still had plenty of wine and beer to drink in the house. Of course they all laughed at me for being boring, so we eventually arrived at the pub. It was a quaint little place, with whitewashed walls and large hanging baskets of cascading flowers. It was a lovely warm summer evening and the birds were singing sweetly as we sat outside chatting. I was doing most of the chatting as usual, I'm sure I get it from my dad.

On the way back to the house, Michelle and Christopher went on ahead as David and I followed quite a way behind. As we walked up the very steep hill, to my astonishment, he took hold of my hand. I insisted we walk a little slower, but did not tell him it was because I suffered from asthma and had fibromyalgia, which makes me very tired and affects most of my body, and at that precise moment it was truly affecting my legs. I think I hide it pretty well though, as I try each day to live with it.

Michelle and Christopher went to bed when we got back, leaving David and I in the lounge. I still had no idea that he fancied me, but we seemed to be very happy with each others company by this time. He told me he liked the fact that I was so chatty and happy as it cheered him up because he was feeling quite low at the prospect of having to leave the Navy in eighteen months time when he would be fifty. He was most surprised to learn that I was fifty-one, as I was then, after I told him being fifty wasn't so bad. Although I know and feel that I look much younger than my years, as all our family fortunately do, it was very nice to receive a compliment.

I was so nervous that evening I actually exhausted myself with chatting, and when I couldn't think of another thing to say it was about two-thirty the next morning. He then got up, leaned over the sofa and tenderly kissed me on the lips. I was so surprised by it I don't think I showed any reaction at all as I was so numb with shock. He asked if he could sleep on the sofa and I went to bed, but I didn't sleep a wink that night. I can remember thinking 'Oh no, I can do without this'. That same evening Michelle and I had been saying it would be very interesting for us to have a guided tour of the ship Christopher and David were on, so David kindly invited us the following day.

It was another sunny day as we arrived at the dockyard on that Saturday afternoon, and there were sailors everywhere. I've never seen so many hunky bodies in one place. Christopher came to meet us with his short blonde hair shining in the sunlight. I was very proud to see him in his uniform, and being tall and a rugby player too, he looked good. It was another ten minutes before I spotted David, dressed in his officers uniform. His dark hair being slightly grey at the sides made him look very distinguished. As I was looking at him coming towards us, I can remember thinking that I must be dreaming it all. It was the most exciting moment of my life. He had a broad smile on his face, just like the cat that got the cream, as my grandma used to say, his sexy brown eyes warming every inch of my body. Yes, he looked so handsome and I felt quite plain with only having brought t-shirts and trousers to wear. We just couldn't keep our eyes off each other the whole time. When it was time to go I had to restrain myself from kissing him on the cheek in appreciation of a lovely afternoon, well to be honest I felt like grabbing him and having a passionate kiss, but by this time there were several young sailors looking in our direction, all with smirks on their faces. However, we did touch hands very briefly when no-one was watching, and I felt that electricity flow between us. You know, the electric feeling you get when you are smitten. Oh help, I thought as Michelle and I walked away from the ship. After walking a hundred yards or so, I looked back, thinking he may have gone below deck or something, but he was still there smiling and waving. My heart was thumping so hard I thought I was having a heart attack. I began to get the feeling, you know the one, when you would gladly wash his smelly socks and iron his shirts without a second thought.

When I got back home to Nottinghamshire he kept in touch, ringing me most evenings when he could. We were both looking forward to the beginning of September when I would be going to Plymouth for seven weeks. We planned to see as much as we could of each other in the first few days of my stay as David and Christopher were sailing for Portsmouth after that. David was getting off there and travelling to London where he was to be working until he retired from the Navy. Christopher was to come back with his ship for a few days before sailing for several weeks. That was one of the reasons I had planned to stay for so long. Michelle had only made one friend since moving in and she hadn't met any neighbours by this stage, so was feeling pretty homesick, although fortunately for her she did find a job pretty quickly.

To explain what happened next, I hope you will bear with me, whilst I tell you about what I had to do back home before I went to Plymouth in September. I discovered about thirteen years ago that I had an underactive thyroid and was on medication to control it. I was told by my doctor to have a blood test every six months and was due to have one before I went to Plymouth. The day before I left I went into my surgery and asked the receptionist about the blood test results and also about a water test that I had recently taken. She went away for a few seconds and then came back to tell me everything was fine on both counts. I can remember asking her if she was sure, because I had been feeling really tired and thought perhaps my dosage might need increasing. However, she still insisted that everything was fine, so off I went taking the same medication.

Chapter Two

Arriving at Plymouth in September, I can remember feeling really hot and sweaty. My legs had been shaking a little, but I had put it all down to nervousness about seeing David again. Michelle was at the bus station to meet me again, and as I spotted her lovely long blonde hair and beautiful face in the crowd, I couldn't help but feel proud. We hugged each other and I can remember telling her how nice she looked in her pretty white top and pale blue jeans. Being five feet seven and a half inches tall, and having a fantastic figure, she always looks good in anything.

That first few days, I saw David every evening and we talked a lot about our feelings for each other. It was very romantic and special. On the last evening before David left for Portsmouth, Michelle and Christopher were going out clubbing leaving us alone at last. I had asked him if he wanted to spend the night with me and although I was pretty nervous about it, it just felt right.

It didn't take me long to get ready that evening with my hair being short and not wearing much make-up, just foundation and pale lipstick. I decided to wear my navy low-cut dress, and with me being five feet four inches and with David being so tall, I decided to wear my navy shoes with just a small heel. With this being the night we went to bed together, I decided to wear stockings and my sexiest underwear as well as my Chanel 19 all over.

Michelle cooked a lovely meal for us all before her and Christopher went out. David held my hand between courses as we gazed at the fantastic lights through the window. As the Lighthouse Family softly sang "High" in the background, we looked into each others eyes and I remember thinking that life couldn't possibly get any better than this. I was totally besotted, extremely happy and couldn't wait until we were alone at last.

Michelle and Christopher finally went out, and David and I held hands as we started to watch a film together. He looked so relaxed in his blue and white shirt and casual blue trousers, then all of a sudden I looked at him and couldn't remember who he was. I started to shake and sweat and felt very frightened. I didn't know what was happening to me so I asked him to leave. He looked at me strangely at first and then he laughed, probably thinking I was joking, but after I repeated it, he phoned for a taxi and left. I couldn't wait to get in bed as I felt quite poorly, but I had no idea what was wrong with me, as I had never felt this way before.

During the early hours of the morning, Michelle and Christopher returned with two of Christopher's mates. They were all being very noisy so I got up and went downstairs. They just couldn't believe that I had told David to leave without any explanation whatsoever. I couldn't understand what was happening to me as I would never do anything like that to anybody. Michelle was quite cross with me as she thought David was a lovely man and that we seemed just right for each other, as I did too. Christopher's mates stayed the night and it was pretty noisy I can tell you. I continued to shake and sweat all night. Then the next day Christopher and David sailed to Portsmouth, and as I said before, Christopher was coming back with the ship a few days later before he sailed to several exotic far off places in the weeks to follow.

During the next few days my memory kept going, then coming back for a brief time before going again. I felt quite ill and continued to shake now and then. When Christopher came back home, he brought another mate back with him. Christopher was rather short tempered with me because he said that he had tried to talk to David to tell him I was feeling ill and apparently David had been quite abrupt with him. I had a terrible row with Christopher after his mate had gone, and with my eyes bulging, I lunged at him like a woman possessed, which was totally out of character for me, as I am normally a kind and gentle person by nature. It all ended with me packing my bags and waiting for Michelle to return from work, poor girl.

She told Christopher that if I went back home, then she would be going with me, so we made up and to this day we have a very good relationship. We made plans to go out the next day as a family and have a picnic somewhere nice. As I was making the sandwiches for the trip, I remember Christopher asking if I wanted any help and me telling him that I was fine. About a minute later I went upstairs and started violently shaking and was so hot that I had to strip to my bra and pants. I must have looked an awful sight, sitting on the edge of the bath whilst being sick in the wash basin. Christopher came upstairs with a worried look on his face and he was extremely kind to me. He and Michelle decided to take me to the nearest hospital because I felt so poorly.

As we drove into the hospital car park, I began to feel really strange. Christopher opened the car door for me and as I got out, my legs went from under me and I fainted for the first time in my life. Luckily, Christopher managed to catch me, he says, before I hit the ground with a bang. I woke up in his arms to see Michelle running towards me with what she called a "bloody geriatric wheelchair". I fainted again as they were pushing me into the hospitals Casualty Unit, nearly falling out of the chair. I was unaware of the other eighty or so patients apparently waiting quietly to see the one doctor on duty at the time. When I woke up again, I was on a bed, in a cubicle, with one nurse taking my blood pressure and another asking me questions. About thirty minutes later, the doctor came and told me that I must have some sort of virus and sent me back to Christopher and Michelle's house to rest.

The next day Christopher went off to sea for several weeks as planned. Michelle was feeling quite down in the dumps and I hated to see her like that because she was normally very out-going. She couldn't wait for me to feel a bit better so that she could have a night out with the friend she had met, as she wanted me to babysit her friends two children, one nine months old and the other four years old.

I felt very tired one minute, a bit better the next, and then I was violently shaking and being sick again. Michelle took me down to the local shops with her later that day. She waited whilst I went in the chemist to ask the pharmacist if he could give me something to help me recover. I can remember saying to him that I hoped my thyroid dosage was correct. He was very kind and looked quite concerned about me. He suggested that I register as a temporary patient at my daughters surgery straightaway and insist on seeing a doctor. As I came out of the chemist I was sick on the pavement. Michelle could see me from the car and looked both very embarrassed and extremely worried.

It was only a short drive to the doctors but I just don't know how I managed to walk from her car into the surgery as my legs felt like they were going to give way all the time. I recall the surgery being very busy, as Michelle asked if I could see a doctor. The already flustered receptionist told her that they had several doctors off ill and couldn't possibly take another patient. The next thing I remember is waking up on the reception area carpet with two doctors and a nurse trying to bring me round. As they were wheeling me into a room, I saw all the other patients staring at me as I went by the waiting room, which was jam-packed. I thought I was going to die of embarrassment. I fainted again and came round to the distinct smell of a very nice aftershave, and looking down on me was a kind faced young doctor. He was very nice to me and after we had a chat, he came to the conclusion that I had a really nasty virus, as they had told me at the hospital. After me telling him my daughter Tracy had rung that day to say her and my grandson Robert had been very sick and fainting too, he was even more convinced his diagnosis was correct and he sent me back to Michelle's house to rest. Much later I was to discover that they were suffering from carbon monoxide poisoning and nearly died.

During the days that followed, each time I tried to venture out of the house with Michelle, I ended up having to be helped back because I kept fainting. I dreaded to think what her neighbours must have thought, and feared that they would think I had been drinking as I staggered around. As the days went by, I decided to stay in bed as much as I could in the hope that I would recover more quickly, but every time I got out of bed to go to the toilet, I just fainted again. I woke up one morning and found I couldn't move a muscle, my neck was so stiff and painful, the tears streaming down my cheeks as I tried to shout Michelle in the next bedroom. After what seemed like an hour, I managed to turn over and get out of bed, but as I made my way to the toilet, I must have fainted again on the landing because I looked at my watch and four hours had passed. I can remember thinking that surely I must be mistaken because people don't faint for as long as four hours. Michelle was feeling quite depressed by everything and was sleeping rather a lot, but I managed to shout her and make her hear this time. I couldn't move again and my neck was still very stiff and painful. My head was spinning as Michelle tried to pick me up to put me on the toilet. The pale green and sand coloured curtains kept going out of focus and I was sick on the lovely pale green carpet on the landing. When she finally got me to the toilet, it was too late, I had already wet myself. Michelle just cried and cried because neither of us knew what to do for the best and I seemed to be getting worse not better.

I fainted a staggering fifty times or more in the

next two weeks and sometimes the faints were getting longer. Tracy rang from Nottinghamshire and told Michelle that as she and Robert were feeling a bit better she had decided to call at my house back home to pick up my mail as I had asked her to do whenever she could. It was lovely to hear her voice, she is a very quietly spoken girl, well, I say girl, she was thirty-two years old then. She has always looked much younger though, and, like Michelle, has a clear complexion, and, although I would describe Michelle as beautiful, I would say Tracy is very pretty and petite. She has always favoured short hair like me, and has it cut in layers to flatter her face. I had missed her whilst I was in Plymouth, and missed her dropping Robert off to stay on Friday nights.

He was eight years old then, and would come running up the path with a big bag of Blackjacks and Fruit Salads saying "These are for us to share tonight, mama." He looked so cheeky with his spiky short blonde haircut, but he was far from cheeky! He had been born prematurely, weighing only three pounds nine ounces. I loved him the moment I saw him, and would spend hours at the Special Baby Care Unit with Tracy. He's always been a tough lad and thankfully he pulled through when he contracted meningitis when he was two and a half years old. Before he was five, he had been in and out of hospital several times, so he was grateful for all the kindness he was shown on the childrens ward, as the doctors and nurses made it as cheerful as possible. I'll never forget the day after his first tooth had come out when he was five. He knew I was helping my doctors wife along with many others to raise money for a new childrens hospital, and came dashing into my lounge telling me the tooth fairy had left him a pound coin under his pillow. I can remember thinking that it was sixpence in my day. I asked him what he was going to spend it on, and he replied "Here mama, you have it, and ask if it will pay for a little window when the new childrens hospital is being built". Tears filled my eyes, and I hugged him tightly, saying "I'm so proud of you darling". My doctors wife was really touched by his gesture, and sent a photographer from the local newspaper to take a picture of his toothless grin whilst holding the pound coin up to his face, although he wasn't too keen on the publicity. His thoughtfulness continued, and when he was six, he decided to go without Easter eggs, and ask for the money instead. His little face was bursting with pride as he handed the £42.50 over saying that he didn't want his photograph taking this time. When he was seven years old, he decided to have a sale in his garage at home selling lots of his much loved toy cars. I was amazed when he handed over forty-five pounds saying nonchanantly, "No publicity please". He also helped me on several occasions when we had tombola stalls at the local hospital, in aid of the new childrens hospital, and was a ray of sunshine to us all.

I had a quick chat with Robert before he handed the phone back to Tracy. She said there was a note on the mat from my doctor telling me to get in touch with the surgery about my blood test results.

It was Saturday lunchtime, and Michelle brought me the phone to ring my doctors surgery back home since there was obviously something not quite right here. As I thought, the surgery was closed, so it was Monday morning before I could speak to one of the doctors to ask what was going on. It was a lady doctor that I spoke to, and I told her about the note Tracy had picked up. She told me my blood test results showed I needed to reduce my medication. I told her how ill I had been, and she told me there were a lot of viral infections going about, and to just reduce my medication in the meantime and I'd be fine. She also said that she was posting me a prescription for an infection I had. I wish it had been that simple but no, things got much worse.

I was trying to hide the fact that I felt worse from Michelle because I thought she ought to go back to work before she ended up losing her job. It was whilst she was at work one day that I tried to get downstairs to ring for a doctor because my heart was thumping so fast I thought it was coming up into my throat and my head felt like it was going to explode. My legs felt as though they were boneless and I fell down the stairs. When I came round, my head was near the phone, and I managed to ring Michelle's doctors surgery even though by this time I was having great difficulty focussing properly. The doctor was quite abrupt, but said he would come.

It was a locum doctor they sent, a tall, wiry looking man with large spectacles much too big for his small face, and as he took my blood pressure and felt my pulse, I tried really hard to tell him what had happened with my medication back home, even though I was having difficulty speaking because I was slurring my words. He cut me short saying he was only there to check that I hadn't had a heart attack or a stroke, and as I hadn't had either, he wasn't really interested in my 'story' as he put it. He quickly scribbled a prescription to help with my fast thumping heart. As he was leaving the bedroom, I started screaming hysterically at him about my tablets as I desperately wanted him to understand what I thought had been happening. As I was screaming at him, he finally got the message, and as he was running down the stairs he was saying "Oh my God, they've overdosed her". It sounded like he fell down the rest of the stairs and just at that moment Michelle came back from work. After she had talked to him for a few minutes, he shouted up to me to stay in bed and not to get out of it until I felt better, and then he left us to it.

I had a terrible night and felt extremely ill the next day, but I told Michelle that I was feeling a bit better each time she came up to see me. I had heard her sobbing during the night and knew she was feeling depressed by it all. By this time I was hearing whispering noises in my head and it felt like it would explode into tiny pieces any moment. I asked Michelle to bring me the phone so that I could ring one of my cousins who was a nursing sister. When Michelle had left the bedroom I spent a long time telling her what had been happening and she was trying to calm me down by telling me to take deep breaths. When I felt calmer, she told me she had to speak to someone about it, but she would ring me straight back. When she did ring back, she told me that from the first day of reducing my medication, the Tuesday morning in my case, I would still continue to feel ill and would probably get worse, but it would take a week before I would begin to feel a bit better. Hurray!, light at the end of the long dark tunnel, perhaps then I could begin to enjoy my holiday and see the sea at last. My cousin was going on holiday abroad that same day, so the following morning, Saturday, I rang another cousin who also used to be a nursing sister. I told her about my predicament and that I had started hallucinating and was feeling very frightened, despite the fact my other cousin had managed to calm me down. She stayed on the phone a long time just talking me through it, but eventually she had to hang up of course. Well, if I'd known what the next twenty-four hours were going to be like, I think I might have killed myself, for nothing could have prepared me. It was simply horrendous and I wouldn't have wished it on anyone.

Later on that same afternoon, Saturday, September the twenty-sixth, I rang one of my friends, begging her to come and help us as I was frantic by this stage and Michelle was really depressed. I told her how ill I was and that it would take her four hours to get here by car. As I was slurring my words, she probably thought I had been drinking, although she knows full well that I never touch alcohol. I couldn't believe it when she laughed down the phone as she said "Are you ----ing joking, I've got a date with a rich businessman tonight". She had only asked Michelle a few weeks previously if her and her daughter could come down one weekend to spend some time with her. I put the phone down whilst she was still laughing, and even thought she might ring back the next day to see how we were, but she never did, well, not until a month later when I had returned home. Michelle and I looked at each other after I told her what had been said and we both tried to put ourselves in her shoes to think what we would have done. We both said that if she had begged us for help, we just knew we would have even caught a plane if we had needed to. The feelings of isolation and fear were quite overwhelming for us both and we hugged each other crying like babies.

I rang my best friend that same afternoon. She

has been my friend for over thirty years, so I thought I would ring her to tell her of my plight. She said she couldn't possibly come because she had commitments, but she did say that if there was anything she could do, please let her know. I felt so ill and feared that if I closed my eyes I would slip into a coma. What came next was simply horrendous, and I know that it will be painful for me as I try to relive it again. If only I had known what peace and joy would come over me just twenty-nine hours later, I would never have been afraid at all.

Chapter Three

That Saturday evening, Michelle and I decided to go to bed early. I heard her sobbing and wished I could make everything alright, after all I had come to Plymouth to cheer her up and for us to enjoy ourselves. I was so afraid of slipping into a coma that I decided to try and stay awake all night. To keep my brain active, I decided to write down everything that had happened to me, starting with my blood test results back home before my journey to Plymouth. I remembered from when I visited in August there was a large writing pad and pen in the top drawer of the dressing table in that lovely bedroom, with the pretty blue and white striped quilt covers, matching curtains and fantastic view from the back window, the bedroom I had been planning to ravish my handsome Naval Officer in. I fumbled about in the drawer for the pen, propped myself up with pillows, and although I was unable to focus properly, I managed to write all night. After writing the first few lines, I was horrified to see something black moving in the middle of the curtains. It was a bats face. I stared in the hope that it would go away, but its wings started forming until they stretched the whole width of the curtains, and then it jumped onto my head with a thud. I tried not to shout out and I wrestled with this creature for a few minutes before it just evaporated on my hair. I carried on writing, and out came another bat followed by another, then another. Shaking with fright, I tried to keep calm, hanging on to the fact that my cousin had told me I would start to get better about seven days after reducing my tablets. The bats eventually stopped pouncing on my head, but I felt my heart thumping so much I thought it was coming out of my mouth, and I tried to put my fist down my throat to stop it. Just at that moment and although I couldn't focus properly, as clear as day I saw a giant spiders web forming on the bedroom ceiling, covering every inch of it. I can remember thinking 'Oh no, not a giant spider, please don't let it be a spider'.

I continued to write everything down as it happened, then to my horror I saw a huge slimy green frog and heard it croaking loudly. As I covered my face up in fright, it leapt from the cobweb onto my head. I put my fist in my mouth to stop my heart coming out, and to stop me shouting for Michelle. All I could think about was I had something to look forward to, because I might be better in a few days time. After several frogs had jumped on my head from the ceiling, and the slime from them had run down my face and gone into my eyes, I fainted again. When I woke up, still not able to focus, I managed to write down 'must have fainted'. Still afraid

I would slip into a coma if I closed my eyes to sleep, I continued to write all night. I was glad the bats and frogs had left me alone, and I hoped with all my heart they wouldn't return (hallucination can seem so real at the time).

As I sat up, scribbling away, out of the corner of my left eye I could see something moving. It was a hamster forming on the bedroom wall, with its nose twitching and long whiskers stretching the full width. As it got larger, the wall began to crack open, and the giant creature jumped on me, followed by several more. Shaking with fright and still sitting up, I covered myself with the quilt and continued to write with the thud of the giant hamsters jumping on me. Just when I didn't think things could get any worse, to my amazement, dogs and cats had somehow managed to get under the quilt with me and were biting me viciously. Large chunks of flesh were being eaten by these nasty wild dogs, and the wild cats were ripping my legs with their giant claws. I was losing blood by the pint, and the pretty blue and white quilt cover was now turning bright red. In addition to the giant hamsters still pouncing on my head, I surely thought I must have died and gone to hell.

I must have fainted or dozed off because the next thing I knew it was morning and the birds were singing sweetly as my head emerged from the quilt. I felt loads of papers all around me and quickly gathered them up to put them in the dressing table drawer. I heard Michelle shout from the landing "How are you feeling?" and I remember saying that I felt much better. She went downstairs and started to get the breakfast ready. When she asked I said I wasn't bothered about anything to eat, so when she had eaten she came back upstairs and asked me if I thought I was better yet. As she was sounding a bit cheerful, I couldn't bring myself to tell her about my night of horrors and just replied I was improving. She went downstairs again for a while and then shouted up to me that she was going to see her friend and, as I was feeling a lot better, she might bring her and her children back to the house to meet me at last. Before I could say anything she was gone.

I couldn't lie down because my heart was thumping so fast and I felt that I would choke, so I propped myself up with pillows and sat up trying to rest as I was really tired. My heart gradually started thumping more and more, until it felt as if I was about to take my last breath at any moment. I must have managed to doze off or faint again, and when I opened my eyes I couldn't see at all. I felt terribly hot and strange, thinking I was going to die, or was I already dead? I just couldn't sense the difference at that time. I thought about my doctor and his wife back home, and although I realised afterwards that my thoughts had been irrational, I remember thinking if I rang them, they might come to see me, but I didn't realise just how far away from home I was. I felt for my reading glasses on the dressing table, hoping I would be able to see to dial. I managed to drag myself out of bed, and made my way to the top of the stairs on my hands and knees. I felt terribly sick and dizzy, and fainted again.

When I opened my eyes, I felt really panicky, because I still couldn't see. I tried to get down the stairs to the phone, but I fell down most of them and I passed out again. When I came round, still unable to see, I felt around me and my head was right next to the phone, which was now covered in sick. Instead of dialling 999, which would have been the easiest option, I correctly dialled the right number, miraculously, of the local hospital back home just feeling for the numbers and asked to speak to my doctor and his wife. I told the lady at the other end I was a friend of theirs, and to tell them I was only forty miles away in Plymouth, in reality it was three hundred miles away and four hours drive. I was slurring my words terribly and didn't think she could hear me, but she said my doctor wasn't there. My head felt really strange, and I kept thinking each breath would be my last. I tried to get up but fainted again.

When I came round, I had no way of knowing just how long I had been out of it, because I couldn't see to tell the time. The receiver was still on the floor as I felt around, and I said 'Hello' a few times, but the phone had gone dead. I can remember thinking the lady I had spoken to would sort everything out for me, as I had given her my name and Michelle's address before telling her I was dying. My hands and pretty pink nightshirt were covered in sick, and the stench of my sweat was awful. I don't know how I managed to drag myself up the stairs again, but to my amazement I did, and managed to sit myself on the toilet at the top of the stairs. I sat there thinking my doctor and his wife would be coming any minute to rescue me and take me home. I started shaking violently and was sick once again as I fell off the toilet seat. The reading glasses I had picked up to try to dial for help earlier apparently ended up in pieces half on the toilet floor and half down the toilet. My head ended up at the back of the toilet and my legs halfway up the wall. Suddenly everything started to go blacker and blacker. I remember having my eyes wide open, and being able to see my toenails going black one by one, then each toe followed by my feet and legs. In a matter of seconds, all my body felt dead and black, and I thought surely I must be dead. The next feeling I had was my heart thumping faster and faster, until it felt like it was coming out of my mouth again, and the pains in my head were horrendous.

Just then, I heard a child's voice outside, and a key opening the front door. I shouted hysterically for Michelle to ring for an ambulance, and not to let the children see me. I had no way of knowing just how long

Michelle had left me until later, when she told me she had been quite a while, because her friends baby was ill and they had to take her to the hospital because they thought she had suffered a convulsion. Michelle's friend, who I had never met until that day, came running upstairs to try and help me, and Michelle quickly dialled 999. I remember screaming hysterically as she tried to get me off the toilet floor. I can remember her saying she was going to pull my pants up to give me a bit of dignity, but when the paramedics finally arrived, all dignity went out of the window.

She dragged me to the bedroom and I remember my head was on her knee and she was stroking my brow trying to quieten me down. I was still screaming hysterically when I heard someone coming up the stairs. It was one of the paramedics. I couldn't see him, but I remember him asking what was going on. I told him I thought I had been overdosed on my medication but felt like I was going to die at any moment. I quickly told him that my brain wasn't working any more, but I had been writing about it all night and for him to read what I had written. As I was slurring my words, I hoped he had understood. I don't remember much else until I heard someone else running up the stairs and realised it must be another paramedic. I heard him say "What have we got here then?", and couldn't believe my ears when the other one said "Oh, I think she's taken an overdose and she's been busy writing sympathy letters all night, haven't you, love?" At that moment, feeling as ill as I did, and with the paramedics getting the wrong end of the stick, I completely snapped. I have never been a swearer as such, just 'bloody' occasionally and 'bastard' when talking about my ex-husband which wasn't very often, but I started screaming abuse at them using all the swear words I detest, and making a few up along the way. I remember shouting "If I had a knife, I would slit your throats and chop your ----ing heads off". I continued screaming vile swear words, and shouted repeatedly for them to get out of the bedroom and get me a doctor, which they did, whilst Michelle's friend continued to stroke my brow and attempted to calm me down.

I was later to learn from Michelle that when the paramedics did go downstairs, one rang for a doctor, whilst the other told Michelle how much sugar they had in their tea. He asked her if I was normally depressed and violent, to which she replied "No, my mum is normally happy and kind". Michelle told me later she had thought at the time it must all be a very bad dream. As she heard me screaming and swearing away upstairs, she realised she had put about ten sugars in one cup of tea, and had to throw it away. As she was making another, her friends four year old daughter, who had been in the lounge with her nine month old sister, came in to tell Michelle that the pussy cat was sitting on the baby. Thinking she meant the white furry toy cat that usually sits on top of the sofa, Michelle didn't take much notice, and asked her to return to the lounge to keep an eye on her sister. It was only a matter of seconds before she came back into the kitchen and said "Ah, Michelle, come and look, the pussy cat's sitting on the baby. Michelle went into the lounge, and to her horror, the Siamese cat called Gizmo, who lived about five doors down the road, was sitting on the baby's face. The paramedics in their hurry had left the front door open and Gizmo had apparently nonchalantly strolled in. It was more than lucky the paramedics were on hand to sort things out, as Michelle's friend was busy upstairs with this strange, mad woman she didn't even know.

Chapter Four

At last the doctor arrived and asked me to tell him from the beginning what I thought was wrong with me. I heard Michelle's friend ask the doctor if he minded if she went downstairs. When we were alone he told me that it was very important to remember everything. My mind was all over the place and I felt like I had been possessed by the devil. That lovely kind doctor held my hand the whole time he was with me, as I flung myself around that king sized bed like a demented camel. I heard one of the paramedics coming up the stairs but the doctor told him they wouldn't be needed.

The doctor had a nice deep voice and I felt very comforted by his manner. It was a terrible struggle for me to think back to my blood test results as I tried to tell him the whole story. Each time I started screaming again, after panicking about going into a coma, he would stroke my hand and keep urging me to carry on talking. At one point I remember telling him I had been screaming and swearing at the paramedics and that I was a respectable woman really. I could smell sick and sweat everywhere and any thoughts of my handsome Naval Officer were long gone.

It's a good thing the doctor was with me on that Sunday afternoon because it was the worst I had been during the whole of those awful three weeks. I remember him taking my blood pressure several times and checking my pulse but most of all I remember squeezing his hand so tightly whilst I was throwing myself around the bed that I'm surprised I didn't break his fingers. When I told him about my cousin telling me I would begin to feel better about seven days after reducing my tablets, he began to laugh as I told him I thought most nurses had more sense than some doctors, although I could still cringe when I think that I dared to say it to him!

He tried to keep me concentrating on telling him what he wanted to know but it was like trying to ride a bike backwards up a steep hill. When I told him I had tried to ring my own doctor to come and help me he said "After all you have told me dear, I don't think that was a very good idea".

It felt like he had only been with me for about ten minutes but I was later to learn from Michelle that he had been with me for about two hours. All of a sudden I began to open my eyes and could see shapes and colours. Very slowly my vision came back, although it was blurred to start with. When I could see the doctor more clearly, he was as I had imagined him, in his late fifties and although overweight, had a good head of silver grey hair that complimented his twinkling blue eyes. I began to feel embarrassed that I smelt so bad and that my hair was wet with sweat. Still holding my hand, he patted it gently and said that it was time for him to go. Thinking he had only been with me for a few minutes, I remember saying to him, half jokingly, "Oh sorry, am I keeping you from a round of golf". He replied "No dear but I knew you were going to be alright when you started telling me of your strong love for your very special grandson and that you would die for him if you ever had to".

I had no idea at the time about Tracy and Robert getting worse with being sick and fainting again. When they had their doctor to visit he told them they were very lucky to be alive. A brick had come loose and blocked the chimney and they had been suffering from Carbon Monoxide poisoning.

As the doctor was leaving he told me to get Michelle to take me to her doctors surgery the next day and have some blood tests. He then said "Oh by the way dear, have a nice bath when I've gone too!!" I asked him how he knew I would be alright, when I couldn't even stand up without fainting. He smiled and said "Just trust me dear you will be fine now". I thanked him for helping me and just felt so relieved to be able to see again.

Michelle spoke to the doctor before he left and then she came upstairs to run me a bath. She took the sheets off the bed and I took my smelly nightshirt off, but I was still worried to stand up in case I fainted again. After my bath I put on a white bathrobe and Michelle helped me down the stairs as a precautionary measure. As we went into the dining room I glanced briefly through the window at the fantastic view and had to fight back the tears at the thought of David and me holding hands just weeks before and that it had all been ruined.

I thanked Michelle's friend for helping me and apologised for all the swearing and screaming for which I felt very ashamed. She smiled as she asked how I felt and told me to try and forget about it all. She looked a bit like Tracy, with her short blonde hair, pretty face and perfect figure. She was holding her beautiful baby daughter, and as her chubby little cheeks raised up she gave me a big beaming smile, so I leaned over and gave her a kiss. She had such a sweet little face with blonde hair and was dressed in a pink dress and white frilly socks. Her sister was sitting next to her doing some drawing and looked up at me as she smiled and said "I've been doing this for you" as she presented me with a picture of a big yellow sun with a smile on its face. She had lovely thick long dark hair and looked older than her four years, as she was also quite tall for her age. Her pretty face lit up as I gave her a hug and said thank you for the lovely picture. Michelle put the kettle on and I noticed that she was wearing the same pretty white top and pale blue jeans she had on three weeks earlier when she met me at the coach station, although it felt like months ago now. We all sat chatting for about an hour and playing with the children had taken my mind off things, and although I felt drained and totally exhausted, I think it did me good. It was early evening when we finally waved them off. Michelle and I looked at each other and both burst out crying as we hugged each other tightly. What an adventure we had had and I still hadn't seen the sea! We were both very tired as you can imagine but I didn't want to go back into that bedroom as I felt I had died in it several times, so I decided to sleep on the sofa and Michelle went to bed.

As I sat on the sofa I tried to lie down but my heart was still thumping fast and it was a struggle to breath with the crushing pains on my chest, so I decided to sit up and watch the television in the hope that I might nod off eventually. At two o'clock the next morning I switched the television off and felt overwhelmed to still be alive. I fell to the floor on my knees and with my arms outstretched, palms facing upwards and eyes tightly closed, I asked God to fill me with Love, Peace and Light several times and to please show me the way forward. I'm not sure where these words came from as I have never prayed like that before but it was the most meaningful prayer I have ever prayed and through the darkness I saw my great-grandma who had died before I was born. She was in like a misty haze and then it parted and I saw my ex-neighbour Pam who had died a year previously. I also saw my Aunty Betty who had died only months ago. I was still praying when I felt myself being drawn to a bright light. I have never ever seen a light so bright but amazingly it didn't hurt my eyes. As I was moving into the light I found myself in my grandparents garden where I used to go in the school holidays as a child. The light got even brighter and then I spotted my grandad who had been dead for about thirty years. It was wonderful to see him again as he had always been the nicest man I had ever known. He was tall, slim and very handsome with his grey hair thinning slightly on top. As he rested one foot and one elbow on his spade and waved his flat cap when he saw me, I noticed that he had an even brighter light all around him.

When he put it back on it was slightly tilted and I looked into his pale bluey grey smiling eyes, which had a naughty twinkle in them. He was wearing an old navy blue boiler suit and as his hand dug deep into one of his pockets I just knew he was feeling for some sweets. Sure enough out came two mints and as we unwrapped them I could feel the warm sun on my face and could hear the bees buzzing as they went from the sweet peas to the chrysanthemums. I smelt a fire smouldering further up the garden and could see butterflies dancing in between the runner beans. At the end of the garden a black and white cat was walking on top of the brick wall towards a pigeon perched a few yards away but the sound of a train scared them off and all that could be seen was a cloud of smoke, which lingered for a few minutes. I remember asking my grandad lots of questions about the garden, just like I used to do as a child. I was really enjoying our little chat when all of a sudden I found myself in their lounge and my grandma was busy sewing something on her treadle machine. She had a bright light all around her. My grandma had died about ten years after my grandad but there she was as real as ever. Grandma had always been a bit over weight and her chubby face lit up when she saw me. She had a pocket in her flowered pinny and out came a sweet for me. The smell of home baked bread filled my nostrils along with the steak and kidney simmering on the stove. Grandma got up to put the kettle on and we had a lovely chat as I nibbled on a ginger biscuit. I remember hearing the kettle whistling and I suddenly found myself back in the garden with my grandparents sipping tea from fine china cups. My Aunty Betty had joined us too and as we laughed and chatted I remember thinking that I didn't want it to end. After a while I felt they were moving away from me but it was me moving backwards. They looked like smiling angels as I put my arms out trying to reach them, but they said "Don't worry lass, it's going to be different from now on, we are sending you some special gifts". What a heavenly experience, I thought as I opened my eyes. For a moment I felt quite disappointed to find myself back in Michelle's lounge and as I got up off my knees I noticed a bright light streaming through a gap in the curtains but when I lifted the nets to see, it was just darkness outside. I switched the light on and noticed that it was four o'clock. I felt so calm and peaceful and very grateful for having had that special two hours with my beloved grandparents and Aunty Betty. I tried to lie down on the sofa but my heart was still thumping fast, so I sat up again and managed to eventually get a bit of sleep at last.

Chapter Five

The next morning I still felt very tired but I was bubbling with happiness. Michelle got the breakfast ready and as we ate our boiled eggs and toast soldiers it felt like I was experiencing food for the very first time. I became quite excitable and kept praising Michelle for cooking a wonderful meal. She looked at me and said "It's only boiled eggs and toast mum".

We started getting ready to go to the surgery and have my blood tests done. I looked in Michelle's wardrobe and spotted some nice cream trousers and a brown top and asked if I could wear them. She said "Mum, you don't like wearing brown and they wouldn't fit you anyway". I washed and blow dried my hair, put on a bit of make-up and went back into Michelle's bedroom and tried on the trousers and top. To her amazement they fitted me perfectly, she couldn't understand it because she was a size ten and I was a size fourteen. She said I must have lost weight and suggested weighing myself. To my delight I had lost a stone and a half during that awful three weeks but I certainly wouldn't recommend the method in which I lost it. Michelle said that I looked really nice and I must admit I felt glowing. As I was still very tired it felt like I had been getting ready for hours but in half an hour we had eaten breakfast and made ourselves presentable.

As we made our way from the car to the surgery Michelle kept telling me to calm down as I was very excitable. In the waiting room I can remember chatting to a lady who had sat down beside me and Michelle nudged me to be quiet. After about ten minutes wait it was my turn as the receptionist called out my name. Whilst the blonde haired lady took samples of blood from me, I asked if I was slurring my words and she told me that I was. I told her I wasn't quite sure what had been wrong with me but it felt like it could have been a heart attack, stroke and Meningitis, all at the same time. She told me to come back in ten days time to see the doctor and said "You take care now dear". I spotted some weighing scales and asked if I could weigh myself just in case Michelle's scales were wrong but it was true, I had lost a stone and a half in three weeks.

When we got back to the house Michelle insisted that I lie down on the sofa and try to calm down a bit as she said I was hyperactive. My heart was still thumping too much to be comfortable lying down so after a few minutes I sat with my feet up. Michelle put some relaxing oil in the burner and then put an Enya CD on. It was called "Shepherd Moons" and I listened to it in awe as if I felt connected in some way. Before it had finished I had dozed off. When I woke up I asked Michelle to put the CD on again and she went into the kitchen to get lunch ready. We only had cheese on toast but I kept saying "What a wonderful meal", everything I tasted seemed like I was trying it for the very first time.

Michelle went to work that afternoon and told me I must rest. She worked at New Look fashion shop and was always buying lots of new clothes. I sat with my feet up listening to Enya again and again and couldn't believe how connected I felt to her music. When I got up I looked in my purse for some reason and found a Flying Flowers card. It started me thinking that with having been so ill and Michelle feeling so down, we ought to have some flowers. I rang the number and ordered some carnations to be sent to us both. As I was putting the phone down an Avon book came flying through the letterbox. I sat for ages looking at all the pretty coloured eye shadows, lipsticks and nail polish. I had no thought of the cost as I gleefully wrote out an order for eighty-nine pounds worth. She was certainly one lucky Avon lady! I went into the dining room, looked through the window and saw two squirrels darting about in the old oak tree that hung over into the back garden from the lane. The sun was shining, birds were singing and I thought what a wonderful world it was. I began to write my thoughts down for some reason and I can remember writing about how beautiful the sun was, birds, squirrels, trees, everything really.

When Michelle came home I told her I was writing a book called "My Wonderful World" or "My Wonderful Life", I can't remember which. She replied "Oh right" and looked at me strangely. I had cooked us some chicken and oven chips with a salad for tea. For afters I did strawberry Angel Delight and was amazed how quickly this pink frothy liquid had turned solid. I had put it in a couple of prawn cocktail type dishes and remember thinking that I had created a masterpiece as I put the finishing strawberry on top. I then announced that I was going to write a cookery book as well. After tea Michelle managed to get me sitting with my feet up on the sofa in the lounge. She lit the oil burner, put the Enya CD on again and closed the door on me as she said "Please be quiet". I sat there and was convinced I was going to write two books; it was ludicrous. I even shouted to Michelle that we were going to be millionaires, just like Del Boy! She came back into the lounge and said "What makes you think that then?" I said "I just know because my angels told me". She shook her head as she was leaving the room saying "What are you on mum?" That evening I had to prop myself up on the sofa again because I still couldn't lie down without my heart thumping and crushing pains on my chest. I was writing for most of the night but I eventually managed a bit of sleep.

The next day we went to the local shops and I nipped into the chemist to tell the nice pharmacist I was writing two books. He sounded surprised and asked if I was feeling better, to which I replied "Oh yes thank you, I'm on cloud nine". When we got back to the house I continued to write anything down from seeing a bird, squirrel, dog or just about children playing outside. I continued to be amazed at the beauty of nature. I rang my friend Paul to tell him I had been ill and that I was writing a couple of books. Instead of collapsing in a fit of laughter, he told me he would help me with the manuscripts on his computer. I also wrote a letter to David trying to explain about what had happened and how sorry I was and disappointed about how the evening had ended.

I continued to be very excitable but Michelle managed to calm me down each time she put Enya on. She also played Postcards from Heaven by the Lighthouse Family but it made me cry as David and I used to listen to it and it also made me sad because I thought I'd lost him.

Chapter Six

It was on the Thursday, 1st October, that Michelle took me shopping in Plymouth City Centre. We had breakfast and then got ready. Michelle wore a pink top and jeans with her hair tied back in a ponytail and looked beautiful as usual. I decided to wear her cream skirt and a brown short sleeved top. I felt very tired but still very excitable. We parked in the city centre and as we entered the hustle and bustle of the city I began to panic about crossing the busy main road. The noise of the pelican crossing, the cars and the crowds seemed really scary to me. It was as if I'd never been shopping before and Michelle had to grab my arm as we crossed the road as my legs felt like jelly.

Michelle made straight for a shoe shop and fell in love with a pair straight away. I told her I would buy them for her and I gave the assistant a cheque. She gave me a pen and asked me to sign my name and asked for my card. After what seemed like an uncomfortable pause I whispered to Michelle that I couldn't remember how to sign my name. She got my card out of my purse and pointed to the signature. After I had signed it I looked up to see the assistant frowning at me in a very suspicious way. As we were leaving the counter a female dressed in white from head to toe came in, she even had white paint on her face and hands and she asked if they had any empty boxes. It freaked me out as I had never seen anything like it but it made me feel a bit better when Michelle and the shop assistant looked as astonished as me. We were quite amused about an hour later when the white figure was standing in the middle of the street like a statue and people were throwing money into a box in front of her.

Michelle wanted some new curtains and we saw a perfect pair for both her lounge and bedroom, which I insisted on paying for. She asked if I was sure that I could afford them and I remember telling her she could have anything she wanted. I've always liked crystal vases and Michelle insisted on buying me an exquisite blue vase. We went from shop to shop and I'll never forget the buzz I felt when I was spending money. I even bought a pair of cream leather shoes for myself, even though they were too big for me, just because I liked the softness and feel of the leather. I was oblivious to the fact I lived from week to week in terms of money, and couldn't even afford to spend twenty pounds on extras. I became very tired and had to sit on a seat outside the Body Shop whilst Michelle went inside. I closed my eyes to try and relax for a moment, and was enjoying the warm sun on my face when I was aware of someone near me. I opened my eyes to find a mentally handicapped young man looking into my eyes with a concerned look on his face. He was about two inches from my face when he said softly "Are you tired?" to which I replied "Yes". He then said "Yes, so am I", sat down very close to me and started chatting. I don't know why but I became very distressed and went into the shop to find Michelle. We both decided we had had enough and made our way back to the car with the many bags we had accumulated. We'd had a wonderful time and even now when I go shopping in Plymouth I always smile to myself as I remember the buzz I got on that day.

The following day we got up and Michelle went to work. I spent the day sewing Michelle's new curtains, and even though I have always hated sewing, I found myself doing a good job and actually enjoyed it! I pleated and hung both sets and then found myself writing again. I even managed to have a rest before getting tea ready. When Michelle came home she couldn't believe what a good job I had made of the curtains and was really pleased. I did a bit more writing whilst Michelle watched TV and we decided to have an early night. I had to prop myself up on the sofa again because my heart was still thumping when I tried to lie down and I still couldn't bring myself to enter that bedroom.

The next morning Michelle told me she was taking me to Looe in Cornwall for a day out. I'd never been to

Cornwall so I was looking forward to it and especially when she told me there was a beach and fishing quay. I got ready first and when I had done my hair and put a bit of make up on I went hunting for clothes in Michelle's wardrobe again. There was such a lot to choose from but I settled on a lovely white lacy top and pale blue jeans. Michelle said that I looked lovely and still couldn't believe I was wearing her clothes. Whilst she got ready I had my breakfast watching TV. There was a programme on about all the horse racing events that were taking place that day, but to be honest I wasn't really listening to it. It wasn't long before Michelle was ready and she came into the lounge wearing a pale blue mini skirt and a pale pink strappy vest with her hair tied back again which was just as well because it was a very hot day.

As we went over the Tamar Bridge into Cornwall I felt a sense of wonder and excitement about going somewhere different and I was enjoying my holiday at last. The countryside was breathtaking and as we passed a house with a swimming pool nestled in a valley I told Michelle that I was going to live there one day but she said I was still very excitable and needed to calm down. As we were approaching East Looe my stomach felt like it was turning somersaults and I burst out crying. Michelle said "Oh my God mum, what's wrong"? I replied "Nothing, I'm home". She said "Oh I hope you're not going funny again because I can't take anymore". We drove over a bridge to the car park and I was still sobbing. As we got out of the car I looked up at all the white cottages, hotels, seagulls, trees and beautiful blue sky. Michelle came back with a ticket for the car and said "Anyway what made you say you were home?" Wiping my tears with a paper hanky I said "I've lived here before and now I'm home". As we started making our way towards the town I felt lots of smiling angels dancing all around me and lifting my every step. The cobbled street from the car park to the bridge was lined with quaint little gift shops and white cottages. As we were walking over the bridge from West Looe to East Looe large fishing boats were tied up along the quay. Pleasure boats and yachts of all shapes and sizes bobbed up and down on the amazing blue river. It was all too much to take in as my angels continued to lead me across the bridge. I gazed ahead in awe as the pretty white cottages, hotels and guest houses towered above. I stopped for a moment as I noticed all the beautiful gardens, hanging baskets and all the lovely greenery and wondered how on earth residents managed to keep their gardens so perfectly splendid with the properties being built into very steep hills. Up and up the cottages went, until it looked as if the ones at the top of the hill were touching the clear blue sky. Even the squawking seagulls added to the magic of that heavenly place.

Walking along the main street we couldn't resist looking in the amazing shops. Some of them looked hundreds of years old and it all added to the enchantment of the place. I couldn't believe how friendly people were and as we passed quaint little streets leading off the main one, I felt as if I knew every little nook and cranny. Oldy worldy pubs, charming restaurants and cosy little tearooms all added to the magic of this Cornish town. After turning left we saw even more quaint little shops, cafes, pubs and restaurants and eventually came to a little car park. As we walked through it we could hear the waves and smell the sea as the seagulls squawked above our heads. After climbing a couple of steps we were on Looe sea front.

No words could ever describe its beauty or the peace that I felt there, even though there were quite a few people around at the time. There were several blue benches along the front for people to just relax and enjoy the magnificent view. The beach was a pale golden colour and very sheltered; to the right a small pier made it's way a hundred yards out to sea and opened up into a circle at the end with seating around the inside. A couple of men were fishing from it when a large red and white fishing boat appeared and made it's way back along the quay. Hundreds of seagulls followed it squawking very loudly as they tried to steal the catch from the dozens of blue boxes stacked on the deck. Higher up on the other side of the river at West Looe, more quaint houses, cottages, guest houses and hotels were built high into the hillside showing off their beautifully coloured hanging baskets and window boxes. Looking out to sea there were all kinds of vessels on the water from small canoes, speedboats and yachts to naval ships on the horizon. To the right of the pier there was a small island called Looe Island. Looking to the left, small sheltered bays and white cottages could be seen in the distance. We walked along the sea front and looked up to see even more quaint little cottages built high into the hillside. Large stones and rocks dominated this area, some people were just sitting or lying admiring the breathtaking beauty all around. We sat for a while watching several fishing boats coming in to make their way to the quay. I could have stayed there for hours but Michelle suggested getting a drink and some lunch at a pub which was nearby. We had a nice chat with the friendly barmaid whilst we ate our chicken and chips in a basket, but all the time I just couldn't wait to get back out there. When we came out I wanted to stay on the sea front, but Michelle said that she was bored so I stayed there while she went to look around the shops again. I sat there taking in every precious moment but I wasn't alone as I felt my smiling angels were everywhere in this, my heaven on earth.

Then a strange thing happened; out of nowhere words were filling my head to write about my last few weeks in Plymouth. I wished with all my heart that I had paper and pen with me so I could have written it all down. After a while Michelle came back and asked me if I was ready to go home but I wanted to stay forever. Reluctantly I got up and started walking away and back down the pretty old street where I spotted a little shop with beaded curtains. I started getting very excitable again and told Michelle it must be a fortune tellers as I dashed inside to hear my fate, leaving my daughter looking quite annoyed outside. It was quite smokey inside and there were lots of TV's on a shelf to my right and a few men sitting on stools reading newspapers. In front of me as I was walking in there was a counter with two men behind it. Oh dear me it was a Bookies!!! Undeterred I asked one of the men at the counter what I had to do to put a bet on. Gazing down at the list of horses names I decided Leah Spear was the one for me and asked the man if I could put £1 on it to win. He laughed at my choice but took my money anyway. I walked outside with my betting slip and told Michelle what I had done. She looked really shocked and then started laughing, out of frustration I think. She said "Right, now can we go home?", but I had to inform her that my horse wasn't running until three thirty and I had to go back to collect my winnings after the race. I could see her getting more angry by the minute and told her to "Chill out", something she was always telling me to do. I made my way back to the sea front again until it was time for the race. I glanced up at Michelle's face as we were walking but she gave me a bit of a glare. We sat on a large rock looking at the aqua blue water and children making sandcastles on the beautifully clean beach. Once again the words flooded into my head to write a story of my recent adventures. I asked Michelle if she had a pen and paper, but when she asked why I told her that I had a voice in my head telling me I had to write a story about the last few weeks. "Oh not another book, don't you think you've got enough on writing your other two", she said sarcastically.

It wasn't long before it was time to go and to Michelle's dismay I called into the Bookies to find out the result of the race. I walked in to see the place was packed and full of smoke. I asked one man if he knew if Leah Spear had won or not. He told me the race was on and pointed towards the screens, but there were about ten screens all with different races going on. I told another group of men that I had backed Leah Spear and they nearly fell off their stools laughing. Before long betting slips were being torn and tossed in the air as the disappointed punters made their way out, leaving me the only one there. I went up to the counter and presented my betting slip to the grey bearded man asking if I had won anything, and he presented me with £33. Jumping for joy I showed Michelle my winnings. She said "What are you on mum because I think I could do with some". We both treated ourselves at a small fashion shop we found near the fishing quay, leaving me with £10 of my winnings still in my purse. We walked along the quay back to the bridge and I stopped to admire all the beautiful boats. There was a strong smell of wet fish as we walked by the fish market and several men were stacking boxes of numerous kinds of fish ready to be weighed before being sold.

As we made our way back over the bridge again to West Looe, there were even more cottages painted in pretty pastel shades built into the steep hillside. I had to stop again turning around and around on the bridge. My heart was aching to go back but I knew we had to go. As Michelle got into the car I had one last look and noticed a boating lake near the car park and a large wooded area where the river still continued to flow. Large Egrets, Shags and Herons were either in the trees or wading in the water looking for food. Tears filled my eyes again as we drove over the bridge and out of Looe to make our way back to Plymouth. I was in love, in love with this Cornish town. I was quiet in the car travelling back, and when we got to Michelle's house I phoned Directory Enquiries and asked for the number of an estate agent near where I lived. I rang the number, told the lady I was in Plymouth on holiday and asked her to put my house up for sale and that I would post her my keys on Monday morning, so she could show people round. Michelle asked "What are you doing mum, where do you think you are going to live?" I replied that I was going home to

Looe in Cornwall, she said "Oh for heaven's sake mum, you can't afford to live there and anyway you have just had loads of work done to your house and made it really nice". She looked worried and rang Tracy to tell her what I was planning. After the phone call Michelle told me I still wasn't right yet and I shouldn't make any hasty decisions.

Chapter Seven

The rest of that Saturday evening was spent with me listening to Enya whilst I continued to write. Eventually Michelle went to bed and I went into the lounge again to prop myself up with cushions. After a while I decided to try lying down but had to get up again because my heart was still thumping and I had crushing pains on my chest again.

The next morning, October 4th, I told Michelle that I was going to her local Methodist Church at Crownhill. I wore a lemon sleeveless blouse with Michelle's black skirt and decided to take my black cardigan too in case it turned chilly. Michelle asked if I'd be okay going on my own but I managed to reassure her that I would be fine. Before I set off I rang the minister of my local church back home and left a message saying I was going to church at Crownhill. Michelle thought it was a strange thing to do and as I was still very excitable and hyper she began to worry about me going out alone. I finally managed to convince her that I was okay and went on my way. As I was walking along I felt so at peace with myself as the birds sang sweetly. Several people were out walking their dogs and I can remember stroking a couple of them and chatting to their owners, even though I have always been quite frightened of dogs ever since I was bitten by one as a child.

When I entered the beautiful church I was greeted warmly and given a hymn book and after saying a little prayer a lady who was a bit older than me sat down beside me and introduced herself as Eunice. She had a kind happy face with short grey curly hair and looked rather posh in her grey suit with a frilly white blouse. She said that she hadn't seen me before and asked if I was new to the area. I told her I was staying with my youngest daughter but that I was moving to East Looe as soon as possible. We got on really well and as we were chatting her friend Bernice came to say hello and sat the other side of me. She was lovely too and as I looked at her kind face and short straight dark hair I thought she would possibly be about the same age as me. As she took her long navy blue coat off I noticed how slim she looked in her elegant pink blouse and blue skirt. Eunice told Bernice that I was moving to Looe, so they gave me their addresses and I gave them mine. We seemed to be chatting for quite a while before the service finally started and each time I looked up a few members of the congregation turned round to smile at me. I couldn't stop smiling to myself all through the service and as I put the last £10 of my winnings in the collection box I hoped no-one would ever find out where it came from.

I asked Eunice if the gentleman taking the service was the Minister of the church but she said he was a Lay Preacher and that the Minister of the church was called Martin. On the way out I passed the Lay Preacher a note I had quickly written and asked him if he would pass it on to the Minister of the church asking if I could meet him. He said he would be happy to, and thanked me for coming.

I said goodbye to Bernice and told her I would see her the following Sunday as she took my hand and kissed me on the cheek. Eunice said she lived not far from Michelle's house, on the next street in fact, so we walked together chatting and laughing like we had known each other for years. We had been chatting for so long that Michelle had begun to worry about me because it was the first time I had ventured out on my own. As I walked through the door she asked why I had been so long because the lunch was ready. Whilst we tucked into the roast beef and yorkshire puddings in her beautiful dining room I told her all about meeting Eunice and Bernice. I remember that on several occasions during the meal, Michelle was telling me to calm down because I was too excitable.

I spent Monday morning working out how I could afford to live in Looe, and I managed to persuade Michelle to take me there that afternoon. I was still not thinking rationally when I told her I was going to live in a caravan in the summer months and stay in an apartment during the winter. She even went along with me looking at guest houses and telling the proprietors that I was a writer, but every now and then I caught her closing her eyes and shaking her head in disbelief.

I remember writing a long letter to my doctor's wife back home that evening, telling her I had been ill and going into detail about the whole episode. I also told her I was writing a book called "My Wonderful World" and that I was writing a cookery book too!

The same evening I wrote to my sister who lives in Portugal with her husband and three daughters, telling her I had been ill and about seeing our grandparents and Auntie Betty when I prayed. I told her I was going to rent a four bedroomed luxury furnished apartment when I moved to Looe, my heaven on earth and that I would write many books before I leave this planet earth! I also told her I had bought a beautiful long white nightdress from Plymouth and after my evening meal I have a bath and listen to Enya whilst writing by candlelight. Apparently I wrote thirteen pages to my sister in all but can't remember much else about what I said. In between writing to my sister, my cousin Diane rang to see how I was feeling and was shocked but delighted that I had moved on so fast, as I told her I felt on a much higher level now and didn't want to come back down.

The next morning I received a letter from my

handsome Naval Officer saying he was very sorry I had been ill and hoped that I was better now. He also said he would like to come to see me when I got home. I smiled as I thought to myself that he would have to be quick because I might be living in Looe, but I was relieved he had written to me. As I put David's letter down, Martin the Minister of Crownhill church rang me asking if I would like to come to his bungalow to have a chat. I was pleased he received my note and I quickly got dressed and had breakfast before walking the short distance to see him. I think it must have been the cleaner who answered the door and showed me into his study. After a few minutes in he came, his white teeth gleaming as he smiled and shook my hand tightly. He only looked in his early thirties with short jet black hair, very dark skin and slim build. He asked me to sit down, and I felt very comfortable talking to him as we both sat on black leather chairs. I told him about me being ill and about seeing my grandparents and Auntie Betty when I had prayed in the early hours. He seemed overwhelmed and told me I was very very lucky. He then told me a very moving story about what led him to become a Minister after living in Uganda. After about an hour his wife came dashing in from the back room, which she was using as a hairdressing salon. She was wearing a long brightly coloured dress in yellow and orange with a matching turban like hat covering all her hair. She too had dark skin although not as dark as Martins. "Martin, Martin", she cried as she ran in the room, "Mrs ------ has fainted, she's not at all well". He got up quickly and excused himself telling me he would be back in a few minutes. Five minutes later he was back saying he had to ring the lady's husband to take her home. We talked again for about half an hour when his wife came running back in again saying "Martin, Martin, no one has come to fetch her yet, you will have to take her home". We both got up and Martin quickly said goodbye and he would come to see me at Michelle's before I went back home.

When Michelle came home from work I told her all about my visit with Martin and although she was pleased I'd had a nice day she was still concerned about how excitable I was. I asked her what was in the carrier bag that she had put down in the hallway and she said "Oh yes, I forgot to tell you I've bought a couple of new blouses and skirts from work". I think she was fed up with me wearing all her clothes after miraculously loosing all that weight in such a short space of time.

We both had a shower and decided to just have a salmon salad for our evening meal, and then once again I started writing whilst Michelle watched the television, although she couldn't understand why I had the sudden urge to write a lot when I had never shown any inclination before I had been ill. Next morning the doorbell rang and the postman handed me a long narrow box. When Michelle and I opened it a beautiful aroma filled the air and slowly I realised it was the flowers I had ordered for us both from Flying Flowers whilst being ill. Michelle smiled and shook her head as she arranged the beautiful multi coloured carnations in a cream vase and quickly put them in the dining room.

After lunch Michelle went off to work for a few hours and I settled down at the dining room table to start writing again. I was convinced that just writing about the beauty of nature and a cookery book about making Angel Delight with a strawberry on top would be best sellers one day. After about half an hour a young lady rang the doorbell and as I opened the front door she handed me a large paper bag and said "Your Avon order, it's £89 please". By now I had mastered the art of writing a cheque and signing it without Michelle's help and smiled as I handed it over. When she had gone I sat down and emptied the contents of the bag onto the dining room table. Out came several eye shadows of various colours, mascaras, lipsticks, nail polishes plus several bottles of nice smelling bubble bath. I can remember thinking what beautiful colours and fragrances I had picked as I put them to one side and continued to write my books.

When Michelle arrived home and saw all the Avon products on the dining room table she said "What's all this lot doing here, I've not ordered it"? When I told her they were mine she said "Mum, what have you done, you don't wear eye shadows or mascaras and the lipsticks and nail polishes aren't even your colour". When she found out how much it had all cost she got really annoyed. As she sat down slowly covering her face with both hands and shaking her head, she told me I must return it all, but I didn't know where the Avon lady lived or her phone number, so I decided to give it to Michelle and her friend.

That evening Michelle told me I must tell the doctor everything when I go the following day to get my blood test results and although I desperately wanted to know why I had been so ill for those awful three weeks, I had felt blissfully happy and full of joy ever since, even though my heart was still thumping fast when I tried to lie down.

I decided to watch the television in the lounge with Michelle instead of writing my books that evening, mainly because she was really irritated with my behaviour even though at the time I couldn't see what her problem was. I tried to suppress my excitement as I gleefully thought about my move to Cornwall and this new life I had to look forward to as well as my new love of writing. The next day we got up early and had breakfast before setting off for the doctors surgery for my appointment. At last I was going to get to know what had been happening to my mind and body during those terrifying three weeks.

Chapter Eight

There was a chill in the air that October morning so I had chosen to wear my pale blue jumper and Michelle's jeans, whilst she decided to wear her favourite pale pink jumper and black trousers. It was only a short drive to the car park at Crownhill and as we got out of the car and walked over the bridge to the surgery, I remembered how I felt when Michelle took me before and I had fainted there. I had barely been able to put one foot in front of the other as I staggered, and Michelle had almost carried me into the surgery. Now I was excited about my future life in Looe and was bubbling with happiness and joy. As we stood at the reception desk waiting for attention I realised I was standing in the same spot I had been in the last time, when my knees had given way underneath me. As I looked around sheepishly I hoped no-one would recognise me but then an impish grin transpired as I thought "Do I really care"!

Once in the waiting room it wasn't too long before it was my turn. Michelle had asked if I wanted her to come in with me to see the doctor but I wanted to go in alone. He was in his early thirties and I hadn't met him before. He smiled warmly and shook my hand

and I began to feel at ease with him. I explained as briefly as I could about my three week nightmare ordeal and about Michelle saying she was worried about me being too excitable now and about my plans to move to Cornwall and write several books. I asked about my blood test results and was told that my thyroid one was now okay but that my blood pressure was high so he wrote out a prescription for some tablets and told me to get in touch with my own doctor when I returned home. I tried to push him to tell me why I had been so poorly but he just said that it was just one of those things but the main thing was that I was okay now. I had another try to find some explanation for it all as I was sure I had suffered a heart attack at the very least but he just said "Viruses can be very nasty sometimes". As he got up and shook hands again he said it had been nice meeting me and wished me good luck with my move and getting my books published. Michelle couldn't believe it when I told her, but after a while she said that I must see my own doctor when I get home as I had been told to do. She did ask me if I'd ever had a nutty spell ever before and not told her about it, but I reassured her I hadn't so she said we should try to put it all behind us now.

When we got back to Michelle's house, she told me how ill Robert and Tracy had been back home whilst I was ill during that three weeks. They had been suffering from Carbon Monoxide poisoning and not a virus as originally thought, due to a brick coming loose and blocking their chimney. Robert had been the worst affected, being a child, and the doctor told them they had had a very lucky escape. My precious grandson and daughter had almost died and I just couldn't take it in. All I can say now is that it's a good job I was out of it most of the time and didn't know what was happening, apart from the fact that they had a virus as had been originally diagnosed, otherwise I would have been absolutely hysterical. Michelle said she couldn't believe it when Tracy rang and told her what their doctor had said, and it was on the same Sunday that the doctor had visited me in Plymouth when I was screaming and shouting as I was throwing myself around the bed, convinced I was dying too. It must have been awful for Michelle at the time, trying to cope when she was feeling low herself, and it beggars belief that I had gone to visit her for seven weeks to cheer her up because Christopher was at sea!

For a brief moment I thought of my handsome Naval Officer and how much we had both been looking forward to spending the night together in September and couldn't help thinking things wouldn't be the same again and that he probably thought I was some sort of nutcase really. As my thoughts turned back to Robert and Tracy's ordeal and the fact I couldn't have been there for them at the time it really hit me hard and I began to sob uncontrollably. Just minutes later the phone rang and it was Tracy, trying to reassure me that her and Robert were okay now and to forget about it.

A few days later my sister rang to say she had received my letter and how pleased she was that I was moving to Cornwall and to follow my dream. I managed to get Michelle to take me to Looe just once more before I had to go home to Nottinghamshire as my seven weeks stay was coming to an end. Each time I had visited Looe it seemed even more beautiful than the last. Fishing boats and pleasure boats bobbed up and down whilst yachts swayed from side to side as they were moored on the river. Windows gleamed in the sunlight on the cottages and guest houses built high into the hillsides as seagulls squawked relentlessly. The charming shops and cafes, and friendly people, were all there as before as my smiling angels led me yet again through the cobbled streets onto the sea front where I was truly at peace and home again at last. Michelle left me sitting on a large rock on the beach whilst she went to look around the shops for an hour or so and I was filled once more with an overwhelming feeling of love for the place which was far greater than I had ever known. The only other place that had come close to me feeling overwhelmed was Matlock Park in Derbyshire where I would sit on my seat, as I called it, facing the boating lake which was always filled with ducks.

When Michelle returned to the beach it felt as

if she had only been gone for about five minutes but she said she had been gone about an hour and a half because she got carried away having a good look in all the shops. She was carrying lots of carrier bags and handed me a pink one which I recognised as being from a very nice ladies shop just off the fishing quay. She had bought me a very pretty blouse in cerise pink, which I loved. We had a bite to eat at the pub very close to the beach and then we had to go. My heart sank as I took one last look at the beach and out to sea where dozens of boats and ships cruised along. I had tears in my eyes as we made our way back to the car. I called into a gift shop and bought about 10 postcards, all of Looe so that I could look at them when I got back to Nottinghamshire.

The next morning Martin the Minister came to see me briefly to wish me a safe journey home and I promised to keep in touch with him. With my case all packed, but bulging this time because I had bought so much during my stay, I took one last look at the lovely dining room where I had held hands with David whilst the Lighthouse Family played "High" in the background, took a long look at the superb view and sighed as I walked back into the hallway to collect my handbag. Michelle had already put my case into the car and was waiting for me to lock the front door for her. I didn't say a word during the fifteen minute journey to the coach station. The coach was already there, and as the driver took my rather heavy case I kissed Michelle and hugged her tightly as I said goodbye. We waved to each other until the coach went round a bend and we could no longer see each other. I had tears in my eyes at leaving Michelle, as usual, and at having to leave beautiful Plymouth and heavenly Looe behind.

When I arrived back in Nottingham, Robert, Tracy and her husband Dale were waiting to drive me back home and it was lovely to see them again. But when I arrived back it didn't feel like home, it just felt like a loose end I had to tie up before I could get back to my beloved Looe. The 'For Sale' sign was up and I stared at it and wondered how long it would be up for sale. Friends and neighbours looked at me strangely when I told them I was moving to Cornwall, so I didn't tell anybody about my plans to write several books.

When Robert came to stay on Friday night as usual he couldn't understand why I wanted to move away, but the powerful feeling I had to move to Looe had overtaken me completely, and I hoped that one day he would understand and forgive me for leaving. I had never done anything just for myself before, and as I still felt the loving arms of Looe waiting to caress me once again, I knew my "me time" had come at last.

My friend who had the date with the rich businessman phoned me, and after a few words I hung up on her. She phoned back a few days later but I hung up on her again, something that I have never done before. I ignored phone calls from my best friend too, although she wrote and told me that her daughter had had a car accident the day I had rung her from Plymouth when I was at my worst so I decided to continue our friendship and she has helped me a lot. My friend Paul, who I used to work with, helped me by transferring the words I had written in Plymouth onto his computer, but although I quickly realized that it sounded silly and mixed up, my determination to write a book continued. I didn't give up and decided to continue writing again. This time it was the letter I had written to my sister and I was going to call the book "Dear Sis". Paul helped me a lot by putting it onto his computer and encouraged me all the way, which I will always remember. My best friend also helped me, and in her lunch breaks she put my first three chapters of "Dear Sis" on her computer at work and also encouraged me. It was about three weeks before I could get an appointment to see my own doctor to tell him about what my poor body and mind had gone through in Plymouth. When I walked in I felt quite emotional as I started to tell him what had happened, although he probably knew that I had sent his wife a letter telling her all about it. I only got a few words out before he got up suddenly and said "Sorry, not convinced, not convinced at all". I felt very upset because I thought with all that had happened to me, my own doctor would at the very least want to know about it. He opened the door and said "Have a nice Christmas", in a very curt manner, even though it was only early November! As I was walking by him, with a shaky voice, I said "I don't want this happening again", to which he replied "Well have a blood test more often then". I just couldn't take it in that I could go through all I went through and my own doctor didn't seem bothered or try to help me understand it. Instead of having a blood test for my underactive thyroid every six months, for the next three years I ended up having one every three months. It was during the three monthly tests that on one occasion I had to reduce my medication yet again.

I continued helping my doctor's wife with the charity work as usual, then one day when I got back home I had a nasty shock as I got a bank statement telling me that I was overdrawn by £500. I went to see the bank manager but he wasn't very impressed when I told him I had been ill and couldn't remember I didn't have any money in the bank. To my relief my brother-in-law lent me the money, a kindness I will never forget.

Every day since I returned home from Plymouth in October, I played my Enya CD that Michelle had bought me, and I had my ten postcards of Looe propped up on the mantelpiece in the lounge to keep me focused on moving there as soon as my house was sold.

Chapter Nine

Christmas day came and went too quickly as usual, but Boxing Day had a surprise in store for me. At 1.30am I woke up shaking, sweating and feeling very scared. I looked out of my bedroom window and my eyes caught sight of the For Sale board outside my house. I was crying uncontrollably because I couldn't remember why my house was up for sale. At 2am, without thinking, I rang my cousin, Yvonne, who was a nursing sister. I had rung her when I was ill in Plymouth in September and I hoped she might advise me what to do. I found out later that she had not been in bed long and had to get up at 6am for work. She suggested that I ring for an ambulance and was very kind, even though I had woken her and her husband up.

The ambulance came and took me away in my nightdress and slippers. When I arrived in Casualty, the place was packed and I was left sitting in a wheelchair with a blanket wrapped around me and was told I would be in for a long wait because they were in the middle of a flu epidemic. I sat there shaking and crying, feeling very confused and frightened. As I had never been like this before I hadn't a clue what was happening to me. After a couple of hours I was desperate to go to the toilet, but as my legs were shaking so much I didn't dare to even stand up and there didn't seem to be anyone around to help. I was surrounded by people coughing and sneezing all over the place and it's a miracle that I didn't end up with flu myself.

It was about five hours before a doctor came to see me, but he didn't seem to understand much English. I tried to explain about being ill in Plymouth that September, but all he said was go home and ring your doctor when the surgery is open. I had no money on me and was told that I would have to make my own way home. Someone kindly phoned for a taxi and I paid the driver when I arrived home. I told my next door neighbour about feeling ill because she had seen the ambulance come to fetch me earlier, but after a while her husband told her to shut the door and I heard him say "They should have sorted her out months ago when she was in Plymouth". I didn't tell anyone else how I was feeling because I thought that I must be going mad. A couple of days later I rang Michelle's mother-in-law, Carol. She had known how ill I had been in Plymouth and, as she was a nursing sister, I thought she would be the best person to come with me to see my own doctor as I couldn't face him on my own with being so shaky and emotional. Carol kindly came with me and had a chat with my doctor, and then I felt able to speak to him. I told him I thought I might be going mad and asked him to make an appointment for me to see a psychiatrist as soon as possible, which he did. I was shaking and crying for the next two weeks, and just stayed in the house so no-one would see me. I was feeling a bit better when the appointment day arrived. It had only taken three weeks, which I was pleased about. I decided to go on my own and whilst I was sitting in the waiting room, I saw several "in-patients" roaming around in their dressing gowns looking like zombies, which worried me. When my name was called, a male doctor shook my hand as he came down the corridor to meet me. He looked in his mid thirties with brown hair that was slightly grey at the temples and he was dressed smartly in a grey suit. I was introduced to a young lady with long blonde hair and was asked if I minded if she was present as she was a trainee doctor. I talked for about an hour or possibly longer as I told them what had happened to me in Plymouth and the Boxing Day episode and how I had been feeling for about two weeks afterwards. He took notes the whole time and then I was left on my own as the doctor said he had to talk to someone. I was on my own for about fifteen minutes and was convinced they were trying to get me committed. I heard footsteps coming down the corridor and in came an Asian lady, dressed in a beautiful pink sari, along with the male doctor and the trainee. When I was introduced to her I discovered that she was a Consultant Psychiatrist. She asked me some more questions and then asked me to go over what had happened in Plymouth again. She then smiled and told me not to look so worried and that she had never heard such a wonderfully positive story. She told me how lucky I was and wished me good luck with my book and the move to Looe. She said that in her opinion I had been overdosed on my medication, and that she would be writing to my doctor to strongly recommend that I have a blood test every three months from now on. The shaking, crying and loss of memory on Boxing Day and the following two weeks was post traumatic stress brought on by the trauma I experienced in Plymouth. She told me that I may suffer from this again in the future but hopefully not. She shook my hand and squeezed it tightly as she said "Wonderful story, how inspiring" and then wished me good luck.

I came out of the hospital into the sunshine and felt so happy I could have punched the sky. Before I left the hospital grounds I went to see my doctor's wife in the charity office, told her about having to ring for an ambulance on Boxing Day and that I'd just returned from an appointment with a Psychiatrist and what she had said to me. My doctor's wife looked very shocked and sympathetic, and she asked me if I was alright now, to which I replied "Oh yes, definitely, I've never been happier". January came and went but in February I was to get yet another shock.

On Valentines Day the usual bills and junk mail came through the letterbox, but amongst it all I noticed an envelope that looked like it had a card in it. I opened it quickly only to discover it was a beautiful Valentines card and it was signed "fancy you like crazy". I thought "Oh my God there must be some creep out there who fancies me", and it made me feel a bit uneasy. I'd had them before and never got to know who had sent them. A couple of days later the phone rang and to my surprise it was David. My heart was pounding as I listened to his sexy voice and when he asked if I had received a Valentines card I was thrilled to learn it was from him. I had never stopped thinking about him, but thought I had scared him off with the September fiasco! We chatted for about two hours and arranged for him to come the following weekend. I was so excited for that weekend to come, planning what to cook and what to wear etc. He rang every night until at last the time came when we were to meet again. My stomach was churning as I heard a car door bang followed by the doorbell ringing. "Oh God" I said as I took a quick glance in the mirror, took a deep breath before calmly opening the door. I managed to get him inside and shut the back door quickly to prevent my neighbour experiencing us kissing passionately on the doorstep, in broad daylight too!

The passionate kiss seemed to go on for quite

a long time until I pulled myself together and put the kettle on. Was it one sugar or two, I asked casually, pretending I had forgotten. The next moment we were kissing passionately again. Several hours later we were both getting dressed with contented smiles on our faces. All I can say is that it was definitely worth the wait! I wondered how on earth I was going to find the energy to get a meal ready that evening but somehow I managed it and it all went smoothly. It wasn't long before we were back in bed wrapped in each others arms once more. That weekend went very quickly indeed but there were to be many more.

He rang me every night and visited me every weekend for about a month and then I had the very bad news that my mum had had a heart attack and a stroke whilst getting up in the early hours to go on holiday to Tunisia with my dad. Within an hour my two brothers and I were at mum's bedside with the doctors not holding out much hope that she would pull through. But mum was a fighter and she hung on. I decided to stay with my dad so that I could be near the hospital to spend as much time as possible with her. Sadly after eight days she passed away after having another stroke. I was so proud of her and the fact that she wasn't afraid of dying. David had been very supportive and came to the hospital at the weekend to sit with me whilst mum had been ill and came to the funeral too. Mum was my best friend and I had often thought how I would manage without talking to her each day, but I found a strength from my angels and I still feel her presence and talk to her to this day.

David and I continued to enjoy our cosy weekends together, but it had been a real struggle for me buying extra food for each visit and I knew I couldn't keep it up. So I plucked up the courage to ask if he would contribute a bit towards the shopping at the weekends. He was fine about it and did help out a bit but after that things seemed to be a bit cool. After another month or so, I began to notice that David had never recently suggested that we go out for a meal or buy me flowers, and it began to feel like a bit of a drudge waiting on him hand and foot every weekend. We had been seeing each other for about four months when he rang one Friday night to say he wouldn't be able to come on the Saturday until early evening because he was going to a wedding. I told him I didn't want to see him anymore and that was that. After putting the phone down I immediately felt liberated, and I had my simple uncomplicated life back again. What a relief, I thought, smiling to myself.

That weekend I spent the whole time resting, watching TV and just pampering myself. It was heaven! I had a few couples come to view my house, but it was to be up for sale for fifteen months before I finally sold it. I waited until a few weeks before I had to move out before I went back to Looe to look for somewhere to rent on a long let. My Aunty Connie had sadly died recently and left me £1000 in her Will, so I decided to use the money to treat Robert, Tracy and myself to a holiday in Looe and Michelle would be able to spend time with us whilst we were there.

It was early evening when we arrived in Looe. I had booked an apartment at West Looe with both river and magnificent sea views. We got ready to go out, and then after our meal Tracy and Michelle went out for a drink and Robert and I sat on the sea front. It was chilly but we were both wrapped up warmly. I noticed there was no-one else on the sea front, and the only noise we could hear was the waves crashing onto the beach and the cry of the seagulls. We sat for a while and then Robert said "Just look at that Mama, the moon shining on the water". It was a full moon that night, and it really touched me that at the age of ten he was able to be happy just sitting quietly and noticing the beauty all around him. It really was a special moment and especially when he said "I love it here Mama". As we walked back from the sea through the cobbled streets, we walked a couple of yards up Castle Street which was off the main street. I stood outside a building looking up Castle Street and said to Robert that I wanted to live on this street. He said he could understand that, as it was so quaint with little white cottages everywhere.

The next day I met the letting agent as arranged

so that he could show me what he had on his books at the time, but I stressed that it had to be in Looe and preferably East Looe. The first apartment was dreadfully dark and grubby, and there was no way I could have made it into a home. The second one was a bit better, but the back garden which was on a slope had washed down into the apartment with the heavy rain and it was in a real state. I didn't panic when the letting agent told me that was all they had available, because I felt my angels were with me and trusted that everything would be alright. Moments later his mobile phone rang and someone wanted to put their apartment up for let. It wasn't far away, just off the main street, in fact just a couple of yards up Castle Street. As the letting agent knocked on the door I realised it was the same door that Robert and I had stood outside when I told him I wanted to live on this street the night before. I felt the presence of my angels all around me as I went from room to room planning what I would do with it when I moved in. The rooms were quite large and light and airy. Off the lounge a door opened out into a small courtyard and I could picture in my mind all the hanging baskets and planters full of beautiful flowers I could look at in the spring and summer. I was so happy I had tears in my eyes as I whispered thank you to my angels. My time had come at last I thought as I quickly said "Yes please, I'll take it ".

The next day Michelle and Tracy said they had

a surprise evening planned for me. I couldn't even begin to think what it was as I got ready that late afternoon, all I knew was that I had to dress up a bit. As we walked down the hill at West Looe, to my horror the road in front of us was flooded with the high tide. It was only a couple of inches deep and we didn't have much choice but to paddle through it, as they told me we had to get to the car quickly because we had to get to Plymouth on time. I still had no idea what was going on but just went along with it.

We pulled up at Michelle's house and Robert and Michelle got out, telling me to stay in the car with Tracy. A couple of minutes later Michelle said that Robert was staying with Christopher, and then she drove the three of us to a car park in Plymouth city centre. I was still in the dark about what to expect as we walked a short distance to the Pavillion Theatre, only to see hundreds of women queuing for whatever it was that was on. I looked for clues but I didn't see anything to give the game away until I saw a poster of Daniel O'Donnell in the foyer. "OH MY GOD", I screeched, "Is it a Daniel O'Donnell Concert?" What a wonderful surprise, as I loved his music and couldn't think of a better surprise to spring on me. I can honestly say I have never let myself go so much as I waved my arms about to the music and sang along with the crowd. Despite the audience being mainly made up of middle aged women, Tracy and Michelle had to admit that they had enjoyed themselves too. It was a night I would never forget.

We enjoyed the rest of the week's holiday very much and I didn't feel so sad when it was time to go, knowing that I would be back very soon living in East Looe. I went back once more to the apartment I was to be renting to have another chat with the owners, and although it looked rather drab and basic, I knew I could make it into something really special.

Once back in Nottinghamshire, I started packing quite a lot of things in boxes ready for my big move. Then to my horror my buyer had a few problems with the buyers of her house, and the whole process came to a halt for about four weeks. I was frantic that I might lose my apartment in Looe and was in contact with the letting agent on a weekly basis. It was all very worrying and frustrating, but eventually it all turned out okay. It was hard saying goodbye to Robert and Tracy but I knew they would come to see me in the summer holidays.

The day before I moved, my best friend took me out for the day. I had chosen to go to Matlock in Derbyshire, and sitting on my favourite seat in Matlock Park, the very same one my mum used to sit on when I was a baby, I felt a peace come over me and knew I would return for visits when I could, as it is a very special place to me. We went to Cromford a few miles from Matlock to see the house where my darling gran gave birth to my mum. Across the road there was the Mill that my grandfather used to own. We stood looking at it in its derelict state and tried to imagine how it had looked in its day. We turned to look at the lovely house again and noticed that it was up for sale and we cheekily rang the estate agent to ask if we could have a look inside. It was a very special moment indeed as we went from room to room taking photographs of all the period features. The kitchen was small and as we went through the back door to the small garden we noticed that it had its very own cave just to the right around a corner. As we entered the back door again we noticed that it said 'Warden' on it in big letters. We made our way up the staircase to a very large bathroom with many period features; it even had an old fashioned chain to flush the loo! We entered the largest bedroom where I had an overwhelming feeling that this was the room that my mum was born in. It had a view overlooking a large lake and I became quite emotional and had to sit on the bed for a few moments to compose myself. It was a very humbling experience and such a pleasant surprise on my lovely day out with my best friend. We finished the day by going to look at the house in Matlock that my grandparents moved to when they left Cromford. It was a very grand, imposing yet very pretty house called Ivydene. My mum still lived there for a while after she had married, because my dad was away in Egypt in the army. I had been born in a private nursing home in Ashbourne and had lived in that very house for a year or so before my dad came home again. As I stood looking up at the house I had only vague yet happy memories of visiting gran when I was a young girl. I had tears in my eyes as we walked away as I felt such a connection and love for that wonderful house and still do. If I ever won the Lottery I just know I would want to buy that house and use it as a second home.

After having a lovely lunch we made our way back to Nottinghamshire, and after entering my house full or boxes, I thanked my dear friend for a very special day as we said an emotional goodbye, and I wondered how long it would be before we would see one another again. In the evening, surrounded by suitcases and boxes, I waited for Tracy and Robert to come and say their goodbyes, but when they arrived it was harder than I had ever imagined. I cried for about an hour after they had gone, even though I knew I would probably still see quite a lot of them. After I had stopped crying, I was filled once again with the excitement of starting my new life in heavenly Looe.

Chapter Ten

The removal men arrived bright and early the next morning and started loading the van. The move was to take two days in all; I was staying the night in Plymouth with Michelle on our arrival and then meeting the removal men just outside Looe the following morning. When everything was in the van, I took one last look in each room just to double check I hadn't left anything, and then said goodbye to my house with a beaming smile on my face. The two men were already sat in the van waiting for me as I attempted to climb into the front with them, eventually the one nearest to me held his hand out to help me in and off we went.

I don't think I stopped smiling the whole eight hours we were on the road. I am quite a chatty person so I had several attempts at trying to have a decent conversation with the two men, but after about an hour I came to the conclusion that they were almost brain dead so I gave up. As he was lighting yet another cigarette, the driver did say he thought I was a brave woman moving all that way on my own especially when I told them I didn't know anyone in Looe.

We made a few stops on the way, but it was when

we made the third stop that I started to get a bit worried. I had asked both of them where they were staying the night and what they had planned for the evening. The driver replied that he was parking the van in Plymouth city centre and then they planned to get drunk. I asked them again where they were staying and they said that they were crashing out in the van. I must admit that my smile did leave me at that moment, when I visualised them being sick on my mattresses in the early hours. I quickly rang Michelle to ask her if she could think of an alternative to this unacceptable situation, and when she said she could sort them out somewhere to stay and that the van could be parked outside her house for the night, relief washed over me and my beaming smile returned once more.

At last we arrived at Michelle's house and she was kind enough to cook a meal for the removal men and give them a lift into the city centre. I was happy because I knew my belongings would be safe outside the house, so Michelle and I just had a relaxing evening chatting and laughing. She did say a few times that she couldn't believe I had actually done it. The next morning, with the rain pouring down, we drove to Looe whilst the removal men followed in the van. Michelle parked the car and then we waited a few minutes before the men started to drive the van down the main street. We watched in horror as the lady traffic warden stopped them when they had only got the front wheels on the street. I had told the removal firm a few weeks previously that they had to get special permission from the Harbour Master so they could park on the fishing quay whilst they unloaded the van, but no, they hadn't bothered to do it. There was no way the large van could have ever got down the main street because the street was too narrow anyway. The traffic warden told them they would have to go through the small car park and along the quay to park the van, and then walk a few yards to Castle Street from there. I stayed with the van all the time in case we got into trouble for being there without permission, whilst the men were coming and going with the furniture. Michelle was busy opening boxes and by the time the men had finished, she had put all the pots and pans into the kitchen cupboards and made a cup of coffee. I was glad to see the back of the removal men to be honest, but to be fair they didn't break anything and were very careful.

I had sold my sofas, wardrobes and dining table before I moved because I was going to buy new ones, so most of my clothes remained in boxes with just a few on a rail that Michelle had kindly lent me. We made up both beds but the bedrooms were cluttered with boxes, unlike the lounge which only had my television and two white plastic garden chairs in it. I must admit it did look rather bleak, especially with the bare floorboards. The apartment was fitted with night storage heaters, which had been kindly switched on for me by June and Don who lived upstairs. It was their son's apartment I was renting as he and his wife had gone to live in South Africa.

Michelle didn't want to leave as she felt sorry for me, but I had assured her I'd be fine so off she went. I had a nice bath, then ran in the pouring rain to a nearby fish and chip shop because I couldn't be bothered to cook anything, and later went to the small supermarket to do a bit of food shopping. I had arranged for my television to be tuned in the following afternoon, so that evening I sat on a plastic chair with my feet up on the other one with my quilt wrapped round me because it was cold and draughty. The draught was even coming up through the large gaps in the floorboards. I just couldn't stop smiling and laughing, and I went to bed smiling even though the bedroom looked like a warehouse with all the boxes piled up everywhere.

The next morning it was still raining cats and dogs, but I was deliriously happy. I walked just a few yards to the quayside and could smell wet fish as the boats bobbed up and down on the water. Only a few more yards and I was standing on the seafront. Although it was a rainy December morning it still looked stunningly beautiful. I was the only one around because of the weather and it will sound rather stupid, but I took a carrier bag out of my coat pocket and put it on a wet seat and sat there with my umbrella up. My angels were everywhere and for a brief moment I felt my mum's spirit with me just as a robin sat on a wall in front of me. I must have been sitting there for ages because when I got back home it was almost lunchtime. I went to the small supermarket only yards away from my apartment to get some bits and bobs which I had forgotten the day before and was served by a lovely cheerful lady called Rose. She was slim with long silvery blonde hair tied back in a ponytail and looked about my age. I told her I had just moved to Looe and didn't know anyone, and a friendly lady who was queuing behind me said "Oh we are all mad down here, aren't we Rose?". She was younger than me by about fifteen years with long brown shoulder length hair and I could see a naughty twinkle in her eye as she introduced herself as Val. We all had a laugh for a few minutes before some more people joined the queue. Now I know June, Don, Rose and Val, I thought to myself and I'm only halfway through my first day in this, my heaven on earth. I decided to register myself at the doctors surgery and was told to sit in the waiting room for a few minutes, and then a nurse would see me to take my details. Looking at all the posters pinned to the notice board, my eyes were drawn to one in particular; it was asking for volunteers to help A.C.H.E., a charity set up by Frank Horsnell, and aimed at raising money for extra equipment for the local surgery. As I already had experience with helping my doctor's wife in Nottinghamshire, I decided to ask the nurse more about it and was introduced to a secretary at the surgery called Pat, who invited me to their next meeting.

When I returned home I tried to get a plumber to come and plumb the washing machine in, but it was another two weeks before I finally achieved it. When he did turn up, he left his tools on the floor near the washing machine, and said he had to walk back to the car park to get something else from the van. Minutes turned into hours until it was eventually evening. I was really annoyed because I had stayed in all day just waiting around. When he turned up the next day he told me he had bumped into a mate and they had decided to go fishing! Still on my second day in Looe, after lunch I had another walk around the town and as I was near the seafront, I noticed the Lifeboat shop and whilst looking at the various gifts on sale I got chatting to a lovely lady called Norma, an attractive, petite blonde lady with a short bobbed hairstyle. We chatted for quite a while, during which time she told me they were looking for volunteers for the shop, so without a second thought I put my name down for a couple of shifts. Norma then told me that she lived just yards away from me on the same street, and I just knew we would become good friends.

When I returned home I sat on my plastic chair in the lounge feeling glad that I was such a chatty person, because it was much easier to make friends. The next few days were hectic; Santa Claus arrived in Looe on the train from Liskeard to switch the Christmas lights on, and I met a lovely couple called Joan and John on the seafront one evening when I turned up for 'Carols by Candlelight'. It was quite spectacular walking through the main street of Looe with the crowds of people all holding candles and singing carols, plus it was a great opportunity to meet even more lovely people. On the Sunday morning I went to Riverside Church at West Looe, and was overwhelmed at the warm welcome I received there. Joan was there and introduced me to a very attractive lady called Gloria. Her and her husband, Phil, owned the hardware shop just around the corner from where I lived, and I knew instantly that they too would become great friends. It was whilst at the service that I was told the Ladies Fellowship meeting would be held on Tuesday afternoon as usual, so I made a note of the date and time. I had been a member of the Ladies Fellowship in Nottinghamshire, and attended church services most Sundays there too.

On monday morning I caught the bus to Plymouth to meet Michelle for lunch and a bit of shopping. I was amazed when it went the coastal route and was even more amazed when the double decker bus drove onto a ferry at Torpoint for the final bit of the journey to Plymouth. It was absolutely stunning to see the naval ships and yachts on the water. I had a marvellous view being seated upstairs at the front of the bus, and it was a very pleasant and memorable journey indeed.

Michelle asked me to stay the night, and the next day she took me to choose some new wardrobes, dining suite and sofas. I had been told by someone in Looe that if I wanted new carpets, which I did, Trago Mills near Liskeard were having a sale in January. So after choosing all my furniture I asked them to hold the delivery until I had the carpets laid in January. A few days later Michelle brought her mother-in-law, Carol, to see me as she was staying with Michelle for a few days. She looked horrified to see the way I was living without furniture but I assured her it would all be worth it in the end, and I just knew that it would look beautiful in a few weeks time when I had my cream carpets down and cherry coloured sofas in the lounge.

I don't think it stopped raining all that December, but I remember having a great time joining in all the activities and meeting lots of lovely new people. One Sunday afternoon just before Christmas, I went to the Guild Hall on Fore Street, which is the main shopping street in East Looe, to hear the Looe Valley singers perform and it sounded just heavenly. It was followed by Don Webb, my neighbour, giving a short speech and then his wife, June, serving warm mince pies, Cornish clotted cream and tea. It was a delightful afternoon and everyone was so happy and friendly. Coming out through the large front doors of the Guild Hall out into Fore Street, it was so beautiful to see all the Christmas lights.

Later on that month a Christingle service was held at Riverside Church. All the lights in the church were switched off, and it was a magnificent sight to see the whole church lit up by the congregation holding candles set in oranges. There were lots of children with beaming faces, and the excitement of Christmas was all around. I wanted to stay in Looe for Christmas on my own, but I kept getting loads of offers to spend the day with various family members. As my mum had died earlier that year, I decided to spend Christmas with my dad in Nottinghamshire. We had a lovely Christmas day just eating, chatting and watching television, as most people do, but I missed my mum more than words can say, and I longed to be back in Looe as well. For New Years Eve, I went back to Plymouth to stay at Michelle and Christopher's house. It was to celebrate the start of the year 2000, the new Millenium, and I was really happy that I had my new and wonderful life in Looe to look forward to. Looking through their dining room window, the very one Dave and I had looked through whilst holding hands listening to the Lighthouse Family album, the whole sky seemed to be alight with fireworks going off for most of the evening. When midnight finally came it was like the sky had gone mad, with beautiful colours and patterns painting the midnight sky. The year 2000 was here at last and I had so much to look forward to.

When the New Year celebrations were over the January sales were on, so off I went to Trago Mills to choose my carpets. It was a massive store, and was packed with lots of shoppers looking for a bargain or two. It was so busy that I decided to just buy my carpets and return home. Within a few days my cream carpets were fitted and my furniture was delivered. When planning the look of my apartment, I knew it would look nice, but to tell you the truth it looked absolutely stunning, just like a show apartment. I was so proud to invite people round. My first visitor was Norma, who I had invited round for a coffee, then June and Don Webb from upstairs. My neighbour, Wally, came round for a meal one evening and my friend Enid, who I had met at the Ladies Fellowship a few weeks earlier called round one day to invite me out for lunch. A few days later another friend Win, who I had also met at the Ladies Fellowship, came round and we spent the day together, which was very enjoyable. I have always found older people very interesting in general, because they have usually got lots of interesting tales to tell. I also had a visit from the Minister of Riverside Church, Margaret Oxenham, and I made her a cup of tea in one of my gran's china cups. Michelle's mother-in-law, Carol, came to see me again with her husband, Brian, and they looked pleased to see that I was very settled.

I carried on helping at the Lifeboat shop, meeting lots of interesting people of all nationalities. Looe is a very popular place and is known worldwide for its outstanding beauty. I was asked by Pat, the secretary of the charity A.C.H.E., to go round all the shops in Looe asking for prizes for a forthcoming event called The Festival of the Sea. I was touched by the generosity of the people of both East and West Looe, and all the time I was meeting more and more lovely people. I saw Michelle at least twice a week for either shopping or lunch, sometimes both. My life had changed so much it just overwhelmed me now and then when I thought back to how my life used to be.

Chapter
Eleven

One day in March I received quite a long intriguing letter from someone called James. He explained that his great uncle was married to my auntie, and that he had visited them both in Derbyshire recently for the weekend. He had noticed a photograph of me and asked who I was. Apparently my auntie had explained that I had moved to Looe recently, so James plucked up the courage to write to me. As he had put his telephone number at the top of his letter, I decided to ring him to thank him for his nice letter. We chatted for at least a couple of hours and I felt I had known him all of my life. He explained he had moved from Sheffield to South Wales a few years previously due to a job offer. He was only 40, but unfortunately he had lost all of his family apart from his great uncle. He told me he wasn't happy living and working in Wales and was off work suffering from stress. I invited him to come to Looe for the day sometime so that we could meet each other, but it was May when he finally felt well enough to drive to Looe.

When we met he shook hands with me and gave me a lovely bunch of flowers. He had a nice smile and a kind face, so I immediately felt relaxed with him. James was taller than I had imagined, about 5'10" of medium build with mousy grey curly hair, and he was wearing spectacles covering his blue eyes. We chatted for a while, then we had a walk around the town and bought some fish and chips back for lunch. James had instantly fallen in love with Looe just as I had done and he told me I was very lucky to live in such a beautiful place. After lunch we decided to go to Polperro, a quaint little fishing village about four miles away from Looe, with very pretty cottages and tearooms and a very picturesque small harbour and beach. As we walked from my apartment to the car it was a lovely surprise when he opened the passenger door of a gorgeous racing green Lotus Elan sports car for me to get into. James asked me if I minded if we had the top off the car as it was a nice warm day. I was really excited as he drove across the bridge out of Looe and was hoping that someone I knew would see me. As we chatted on the way to Polperro I asked him how old he was, and he told me he was in fact 13 years younger than me. We had a lovely afternoon and returned to Looe to have a delicious cream tea at a tea room just a few yards from where I lived. When it was time for James to go home he asked if he could visit again. It had been a pleasure meeting him and I knew I had made a friend for life.

My dad came to stay in April and enjoyed it very much. I continued to do my charity work, meeting new people and generally loving my time in Looe. Then in

June that year it was The Festival of the Sea and I was busy doing my bit for the charity A.C.H.E. We had been given a large tent for the tombola stalls, but it was so windy that the tent collapsed and we ended up putting all the stalls in the empty fish market. Tombola stalls, skittles and coconut shies where just a few of the many attractions that were on offer. I was given the job of standing on the quayside asking people as they neared the fish market if they would like to buy a tombola ticket and generally join in the fun. The town was buzzing with holiday makers and it was easy selling the tickets. Most of the A.C.H.E. helpers wore t-shirts or sweatshirts with 'The Festival of the Sea' written on the front. My sweatshirt was navy blue with yellow writing on it. A few locals were dressed as pirates or wenches, and I believe there were lots of activities taking place on the sea front and beach, including a display put on by the Lifeboat crew. I enjoyed every minute of that weekend and it was very special indeed and very rewarding. A few days later I sadly found out my dear gran had passed away in Buxton at the age of 101.

In August Tracy and Dale came to stay along with my grandson, Robert. It was a lovely couple of weeks and they all fell in love with Looe immediately. The weather was gorgeous so they were able to go on the beach for most of the holiday. I treasured every moment I spent with Robert and was sad when they had to go home. I was pleased when they told me they would be coming to Looe for the New Years Eve celebrations and I soon settled back into my lovely relaxed life in Looe. A week after they had gone home, James came down to stay with me for a weeks holiday. He had visited for an occasional week-end after our first meeting and we were the best of friends by then. Michelle and lots of my friends in Looe who had met James were making comments about us being a lovely couple. I thought it was quite amusing because we were just good friends, and with him being a lot younger than me anyway, I had no thoughts of romance at all.

After his arrival, we were having a meal together when James told me he had a few photos of his great uncle and my auntie's wedding, but he didn't know some of the people on the photos and wondered if I might recognise them. When I looked at them I was astounded. They were group photographs with his great uncle and my auntie, his gran and grandad, my mum, dad and gran, plus me when I was about 13 years old, standing with my sister and brother, Ron. I was even more amazed when James told me his mum was pregnant with him at the time and only attended the following reception in Hathersage , so in a way James was there too! We sat at my dining table just staring at the photos whilst shaking our heads and smiling at each other – Wow! Was it fate that had brought us together I wondered or perhaps our angels.

We had a nice week, and with James having a car it was nice to see a lot more of Cornwall. Towards the end of the week he told me he was dreading going back home to Wales, but reluctantly he had to go. He gave me a lovely hug and kiss on the cheek as he thanked me for a wonderful holiday.

I settled back into my life in Looe but found myself thinking of James most of the time. He had so many wonderful qualities about him; kindness, good manners, integrity, empathy, honesty, to name just a few. When he rang me each week as usual, I noticed something had changed in me. I was excited to hear his voice and looked forward to seeing him again. I was missing him like mad and my heart was beating fast when I heard his voice. I was falling in love with a wonderful man, but I dare not show it because I didn't want to spoil our friendship and anyway I was too old for him.

September came and went very quickly and James and I had found our telephone conversations changing quite a bit because we had started flirting with each other. Nothing too much, just subtle comments here and there. He was suffering from stress again with his job as an engineer but his heart was still in Looe. One evening whilst chatting to each other on the phone, I told him that he was in a good position financially to buy a small apartment in Looe for cash if he was still unhappy in Wales, without initially selling his flat in Wales if he wanted to. I was sad thinking of him being so unhappy, and thought it might give him another option to think about as he felt he was in a rut.

In October James came to stay with me for a week-end and I had asked him if he wanted to look at a few places for sale in Looe, just to cheer him up. When he agreed I was quite surprised, so off we went to view apartments and cottages. The first few apartments were not suitable for him, as they were quite run down and not appealing at all. A couple of cottages were nice but too small, so then for the final viewing we went up to the Barbican area of East Looe at the top of a steep hill. It was very pleasant up there with magnificent views of East and West Looe. As we got out of the estate agents car we immediately had a good feeling for the area, and when we went inside the beautiful apartment it was just perfect for him. When we got back to my apartment we had a coffee and James didn't say much at all and looked deep in thought. I said to him that with him being so unhappy with his job and living in Wales he could, if he wished, change his life like I had done and make the big move. With the apartment being vacant and him being fortunate enough to be able to buy it for cash, I had said to him that he could give his notice in at work over the phone and stay with me until he moved into the new apartment in about six weeks time, if he wanted to. It was up to him, but I had just pointed out the possibilities to him, and couldn't do anymore for him except be a good listener when he was feeling down.

James went out to buy a newspaper at my local newsagents, and whilst he was out I was thinking how nice it would be if he only lived just up the hill from me, and how much happier he would be if he only had the courage to make that decision. Deep down I didn't think he would give it a second thought and come Sunday evening, I just knew I would be waving him goodbye again, and worrying about him feeling low at the prospects of going back to Wales. I decided not to say anymore about the nice apartment we had just viewed and started preparing lunch. A few minutes later as I was laying the dining table, James walked in, put his newspaper on the table and said "Right, I've made a decision and I'm buying that lovely apartment we have just seen, I've put an offer in for it, I'm giving my notice in at work on Monday morning and will you marry me?" He then produced a large bunch of flowers from behind his back as he kissed me tenderly on the cheek. Wow! What a shock, but even though I said I would never marry again I said yes and gave him a big hug which turned into a long lingering kiss. After lunch we went a walk to the sea front holding hands and I don't think either of us stopped smiling. The sun was shining on the sea as James told me he loved me, to which I replied tenderly "I love you too". I couldn't believe it was happening; we were in love.

On the Monday morning, I gave six weeks notice in writing to June upstairs and told her our news. She was delighted and happy for us but said she was sad because I would be leaving the apartment. Michelle, Tracy and Robert were very happy for us, as all my family and our friends were. James' Great Uncle Johnny and my auntie were delighted to hear the news; after all, if my photo hadn't have been on display in their house, James and I might never have met. That same Monday morning we drove to South Wales, and James gave his notice in at work saying he would not be working it because he was moving to Cornwall. Afterwards we drove to a nearby beauty spot, and at the top of a hill looking down on a reservoir with birds singing sweetly and the sun shining warmly, James put his arms above his head and said "I'm free". Then with a beaming smile on his face, he picked me up and swung me round and round saying "Thank you, Thank you". It was a joy to see him so happy and a moment we will never forget. On our return to Looe, we went out for a lovely romantic meal in the evening and slept together for the first time, although to be honest I don't think we did much sleeping!

The next day we went to Plymouth and James bought me a beautiful solitaire diamond ring, and we also looked at wedding rings for our forthcoming wedding, which was to be on Valentines Day the following year, only four months away. The next six weeks passed quickly until our moving day arrived, and it was a year to the day that I first moved to Looe. I had in fact expected to live in my first apartment for several years, and could never have guessed when I first moved to Looe that in the space of a year so much could have happened to me. It had been a magical year, the year 2000, although it was sad when my dear gran passed away in June.

We settled in our new apartment with ease and James decided not to look for a job until after we came back from honeymoon. I had never seen him looking so well and happy. In between planning our wedding day, we had lots of happy days out just exploring Devon and Cornwall. It was like a long holiday and just what James had needed to make him completely well again after all the stress he had been suffering from. As for me, well, I had to pinch myself most days because it was like living a fairytale.

Christmas 2000 was a very happy occasion because it was our first Christmas together. James and I had enjoyed the build up to it as we joined in all the activities down in the town, just as I had done the previous December. We spent New Years Eve at Michelle and Christopher's house with their dog, Daphne, an adorable English bull terrier, along with my brother, Ron, his partner Mylena and my lovely niece, Bessie, all enjoying a meal together whilst watching the fireworks from their dining room window. It seemed like a lifetime ago when I held hands with my Naval Officer looking through that same window, and yet here I was with my lovely future husband and blissfully happy!

Chapter Twelve

On the eve of our wedding, family and friends settled in at the hotel we had chosen for our reception. My dad, sister and youngest brother couldn't make it to the wedding, which was to be a small affair. It was lovely to see family and friends all laughing and chatting whilst having a drink together. I had been looking forward to seeing Robert and Tracy because I had missed them so much, even though I had seen them in August for a holiday, and when James and I had visited them in Nottinghamshire only a few weeks previously.

Our big day had arrived and the sun was shining brightly just as I knew it would. The wedding was at 2.00pm so we had lots of time to get ready. James' friend Jan turned up first; he had kindly agreed to us using his old green Volvo car to drive to the church and was smartly dressed in a grey suit. He was tall and handsome with grey hair, and looked younger than he was which was in his early fifties like myself. My brother Ron was the next to arrive at our apartment together with his partner Mylena and their daughter Bessie. Ron was wearing a dark suit and looked very smart and handsome as usual. His partner Mylena is very petite and was dressed in a lovely bluey grey skirt and jacket with her naturally curly chestnut hair down to her shoulders. When I spotted Bessie I nearly cried; she was to be my bridesmaid and looked beautiful with her blonde hair done up in soft curls. She was wearing a full length ivory long sleeved silk dress trimmed with ivory fur, along with ivory satin shoes and carrying a posy of cream roses. Although she was only eight years old, she looked at least twelve with just a touch of lipstick on. Just at that moment, James came out of the bedroom to greet them. I know you're not supposed to see the groom until you get to the church as it's bad luck but we weren't superstitious. He had been to have his hair cut short a week before the wedding, and it suited him a lot better as it didn't look curly anymore. He was dressed in a navy Yves Saint Laurent suit with an ivory shirt and his tie was a mixture of navy, cream and light yellow check. I've never seen him look so lovely and thought how lucky I was to be marrying such a wonderful man.

Michelle, Tracy and Robert called in to see us on their way to the church. Robert looked very nice in his cream coloured trousers and pullover together with a navy shirt. Tracy looked gorgeous in a brown straight dress to the knee and a lovely cream jacket, and Michelle looked stunning as well in a pale blue trouser suit. James' best man, Martyn, popped in briefly looking smart in a dark suit, then he and James went to the church with Jan driving his old green car as promised trimmed with ivory ribbons. Ron sat in our lounge reading the newspaper and as I was still not dressed yet I shouted Bessie to come into my bedroom to help me and have a chat. I had done my hair earlier that morning and after several attempts at putting cream rose buds in, I had given up on them and decided to just leave my hair without them. I put on my long satin ivory straight skirt with a split up the back and then put on my cream, gold and ivory bodice. My pale gold strappy shoes were soon on along with my ivory chiffon stole draped around my shoulders.

My heart began to beat quite quickly when I saw Jan's car arriving back from the church. Picking up my bouquet of cream roses from my dressing table, I took a deep breath and held Bessie's hand as we came out of the bedroom. Ron, Bessie and I all piled into Jan's car for the five minute journey to Riverside Church.

As we pulled up outside the church at West Looe I noticed the sun shining on the sparkly blue river as the boats bobbed up and down. A few friends and neighbours were gathered outside smiling and waving at us. The archway to the church had been decorated with white flowers by some of the members and I became quite emotional when some of the stewards greeted me with lots of compliments. As Ron walked me down the aisle with Bessie close behind us and the wedding march playing, I noticed heads turning from both sides of the church and felt very happy that so many family and friends from far and wide had come to share our special day. There were many friends from the church, but most important to me was that my friends from the Ladies Fellowship were there giving me encouraging smiles and waves. I had picked my favourite hymns, 'Guide Me O Thou Great Jehovah' and 'Love, Divine, All Loves Excelling', and with some of James' friends being good Welsh singers, together with members of the church, the whole church came alive with the powerful music.

I was happy that the Reverend Margaret Oxenham was able to conduct the service and that my friend, Jean Dingle, was playing the organ. It was a wonderfully moving service, and during it all I felt my mum's spirit with me and my angels too. Hand in hand with my husband, we walked back down the aisle smiling at all our family and friends. As we stood outside the church for the photos to be taken, the sun was warming my bare shoulders and magically lighting up the river and I felt overwhelmed with happiness.

As most of our guests walked over the bridge to the hotel for the reception at East Looe, James and I along with Bessie and Jan drove up to Hannafore. It was only a short distance, and well worth it as the sea views stretched for miles. We had quite a few photographs taken on the beach at Hannafore, with Looe Island in the background, and we were lucky because the sun was still shining down on us. I looked up once or twice at Jan standing by the car eating Quality Street and remembered that we still had our reception to look forward to.

After a while, Bessie and I started to feel a bit chilly, so we made our way to the car and travelled the short distance to the hotel. As we entered the main doors, we were greeted with champagne, and Tracy, Michelle and Robert were waiting to take photographs of us as we held up our glasses. Everywhere looked fantastic with cream flowers and large gold helium balloons attached to the tables in the pretty dining room. We only had thirty five guests at the reception, so we were all able to sit at the tables looking out over the river just across the road. We all had such a happy time and the day passed far too quickly. At 11.30pm, James and I went back to our apartment whilst the rest of our guests stayed the night at the hotel. James and I were so tired we just went to sleep in each others arms feeling very content.

The next morning we went back to the hotel to wave everyone off. Bessie was crying because she didn't want to go and told me she had enjoyed it all so much she just wanted us all to be together for ever. When Ron phoned later to say they were back home safely, he said Bessie had cried all the way back home to Nottingham. It was hard saying goodbye to Tracy and Robert, but we knew we would be seeing them again in August. When we had said all our goodbyes to our guests, James and I walked through the town to the seafront. It was another warm day as the reflection of the sun shone on each rippling wave and looked like silver butterflies dancing on the water. Everywhere looked so magical and I thought to myself that I will write a book one day about how I came to be living in this magical place, and call it Smiling Angels.

A few days after the wedding we went on a two weeks all inclusive holiday at a five star hotel in the Dominican Republic. We enjoyed every moment of that wonderful honeymoon with the magnificent scenery, scrumptious food and friendly people and vowed to go back there one day. On our return home I couldn't wait to walk through the streets of Looe again and onto the seafront once more. It was whilst we were walking along Fore Street that I stopped for a moment and told James if I ever wanted a part-time job I would like to work there, and I pointed to a quaint and charming little gift shop. It was at that moment we spotted a notice on the door saying staff were required. Without a second thought I went inside to enquire, and was lucky that the owner was upstairs at the time, and able to interview me straightaway. A lovely young woman in her early thirties with short black shining hair and a beautiful smile that lit up the room introduced herself as Susannah. I immediately felt at ease with her, and within minutes was told I had the job if I wanted it. I still work there now, just at the weekends, and love meeting people from all over the world. I am very fortunate to have the best employers ever in Susannah and Andrew Gill. They are so kind and understanding and also extremely thoughtful.

James got a job as a receptionist in a large hotel at about the same time. Tracy, Dale and Robert came to see us in August that year, and whilst they were here we decided to get a cat from the Cats Protection League. We drove to St Cleer, a few miles away, to a charming house with an enchanting garden and we met Maureen and John who were fostering some cats for the Cats Protection League. We walked with them to a large barn down a track where we could hear a rippling stream and see some horses grazing in a nearby field. John opened the barn doors and we immediately saw some white goats in an enclosure. After stroking them, our eyes were drawn to a large pen with several cats roaming round and miaowing loudly. On entering the pen we were told the names of about five cats as they brushed up against our legs purring, but I was drawn to a small black and white cat in a cardboard box higher up on a ledge. John said her name was Charlie, but we would be wasting our time with her because she was too timid. We must have stood in that barn for about an hour and all the time I was stroking Charlie and whispering to her. She just looked like the black and white cat on the Felix advert, only she was more beautiful. Although she was in a cardboard box, she looked so regal yet unhappy and sad. After about an hour I said to James "I want this one", and whispered to Charlie that we were coming back for her soon and gave her a kiss. A few days later Maureen and John came to our apartment to bring Charlie. She was still quite small even though she was a year old. She had been born on the moors to a feral cat, and was lucky enough to be found and taken in by the Cats Protection League. We had been told that Charlie was an indoor cat, and she seemed very happy chattering to the birds through the window, and soon settled in with us.

We lived very happily in our apartment for the next five years. June and Don Webb, the kind couple from above my first apartment, sadly died during that time and I still think of them often for the warmth and support they both gave me when I was living on my own. In 2005 we decided to buy somewhere detached and fell in love with Cherry Tree Cottage, a charming pale pink cottage just down the road from where we lived but closer to the sea and town. It has a small garden to the front with a large flowering cherry tree, and the back garden is very enchanting and private. Charlie goes out now when she feels like it and it's only a matter of time before she catches one of the many birds that visit our garden.

Sadly my dad died in February 2006. In August of the same year Tracy, Dale and Robert came to live nearby, so we are very fortunate to have both our daughters and grandson around us. James and I are extremely happy here and have no wish to move again as we have found our dream place. Our dear friend Win came to visit us shortly after we had moved, but sadly passed away at the grand old age of 97 later the same year.

James is very supportive and I still can't believe how kind he is. I will be celebrating my 60th birthday in May 2007, and I thank my angels every day for bringing me to Looe. It truly is my heaven on earth, not a bad place to be if you can find it. If you find you need help in your life, why not try saying a meaningful prayer or ask your angels? You never know what might happen!